That's Just the Way It Works

THAT'S JUST THE WAY IT WORKS

A Practical Look at Biblical Wisdom

Ronald E. Lovins

XULON PRESS

Xulon Press
2301 Lucien Way #415
Maitland, FL 32751
407.339.4217
www.xulonpress.com

© 2023 by Ronald E. Lovins

All rights reserved solely by the author. The author guarantees all contents are original and do not infringe upon the legal rights of any other person or work. No part of this book may be reproduced in any form without the permission of the author.

Due to the changing nature of the Internet, if there are any web addresses, links, or URLs included in this manuscript, these may have been altered and may no longer be accessible. The views and opinions shared in this book belong solely to the author and do not necessarily reflect those of the publisher. The publisher therefore disclaims responsibility for the views or opinions expressed within the work.

Unless otherwise indicated, Scripture quotations taken from the King James Version (KJV)–*public domain.*

Paperback ISBN-13: 978-1-66287-293-8
Ebook ISBN-13: 978-1-66287-294-5

This book is dedicated to
Julianne, my loving, faithful wife
Christy and Jay Tate, my daughter and son-in-law
Michael and Natalie Lovins, my son and daughter-in-law
And all my grandchildren.

TABLE OF CONTENTS

Preface ix

Introduction xiii

Chapter 1 – The Wisdom of Solomon 1

Chapter 2 – The Power of Observation................... 10

Chapter 3 – How I Became an Observer 18

Chapter 4 – Life Is Hard 30

Chapter 5 – Knowledge, Understanding, and Wisdom....... 35

Chapter 6 – Wisdom, the Principal Thing 42

Chapter 7 – The Flow of Creation 51

Chapter 8 – Understanding the Flow of Spiritual Things 58

Chapter 9 – Judgment vs. Consequences................... 69

Chapter 10 – Spirit, Soul, and Body 81

Chapter 11 – What about Jesus? (Spirit, Soul, and Body Continued)................................. 92

Chapter 12 – Being an Overcomer (Part One)............. 102

Chapter 13 – Being an Overcomer (Part Two)............. 111

Chapter 14 – Promise or Principle?..................... 120

Chapter 15 – Wisdom Alone Is Not Enough..............132

Chapter 16 – Only by the Grace of God..................140

Chapter 17 – The Big Picture 149

Chapter 18 – Wisdom for YOUR Life 158

Chapter 19 – The Conclusion of the Whole Matter 170

Chapter 20 – And Finally … 175

PREFACE

I could write a book! I wonder how many of us have said that. I know I've said it many times, not ever really thinking I would. I may have had a good idea of what the subject, the title, and maybe the first sentences would be. But what about all the remaining chapters? Would my writing be coherent? Readable? Interesting to others? Who would read it? Would I just end up looking foolish?

Think about all the people who have written books and paid to have them published just to end up with cases of unsold, unread books taking up valuable attic space. What would an author do with such a collection? Leave it up to the kids to dispose of after he or she has passed from this life?

So, even though I have thought about it for several years, what is it that makes me think I can beat the odds? With so many bookstores and thousands of books lining the shelves it's no wonder that people say they could write a book but never do.

So, here I am, writing a book. Even I find that hard to believe.

Some time ago while sitting at my computer on a Sunday afternoon, the thought occurred to me that I had something I needed to say that others might need to read, so I may as well get started. So I did.

I feel I should mention that my education, experience, and credentials are not remarkable in any way. I'm just an ordinary minister who has lived a long time. But I'm also an avid observer of life, of people, and of things that affect us all. I always try to understand and explain to others why things are the way they are. To say that

I've figured it all out would be a gross distortion of what I think of myself and my grasp on life's issues. As I've said many times, I have far more questions than answers.

A few years ago I stumbled onto some scriptures that have helped me to make sense out of many of life's puzzles. Whether or not others will find my understanding of these scriptures (which I will present in my introduction) to be believable, acceptable, true, and helpful, only time will tell. The last thing I want to do is come across as some kind of kook or know-it-all who has conjured up some outlandish, left-field "revelations" that are completely out of the mainstream of solid Christian thinking. There already is more than enough of that.

I'm a preacher, not a theologian. It is not my intention to create a new doctrine based on my opinions as presented here. I try never to judge others by what I think. It is my hope, however, that people who read this book will come away with a better understanding of themselves, their spiritual/physical make-up, and how these things affect their relationship with God. I would like readers to realize there are specific reasons that things work the way they do, and when we align ourselves with those principles, life tends to be better in every way.

This book will contain no Greek or Hebrew word studies. There will be no effort to convince people of various denominations that my doctrine is right and theirs is wrong. This book is not a doctrinal manual. It is simply a practical look at the wisdom of God and how it can be applied to anyone's life. My hope is that virtually any Christian of any denomination will be able to understand some things about themselves and the world in which we live in a better, more productive way.

PREFACE

To anyone who chooses to read this book, please accept my gratitude for even considering these thoughts. May you be blessed as you read.

Oh, one more thing. In this book, I will often use the words *I*, *me*, *in my view*, and the like. Please don't think of these as an indication of self-centeredness or arrogance. It is just an attempt to express the views as my own and not necessarily those of anyone else. And, although the ideas contained in this book are mine, I never feel as though my word is the last word on anything. Feel free to dissect my thoughts, pick them apart, and disagree with them. I am writing because what I feel I have learned has been a big help to me. Maybe it will be to you as well.

Again, thank you for reading.

Introduction

Questions, questions, questions. Is there no end to the questions? Where is God when I need him? Why do bad things happen to good people? Why do good things happen to bad people? The Bible says that if I asked, I would receive. I asked, but I didn't receive. Why is that? I thought that when a person serves God, life is supposed to be problem free. So why do I have so many problems? If I must deal with some of the same problems that non-believers deal with, then what is the point?

Maybe you've asked some of these very questions. They are quite common; as a minister, I've heard them asked many times. Full disclosure: I may have asked some of them myself.

Here are some general subjects that give rise to questions that have been pondered, discussed, explored, and studied since the beginning of time.

~Life~
How long would it take to exhaust this topic?
The effort would be never-ending and would
quickly become quite boring.

~Truth~
How many times have you heard that age-old question, "What is truth?" Normally, when it is asked, it is not intended to engender an answer or even much of a discussion. And if it did, it could very well degenerate into a full-blown argument won by no one.

~Why~

Who knows why? It is a question that can go on into infinity and never arrive at a conclusion.

These and other questions weigh heavily on people's minds from time to time. There are unending thoughts, opinions, beliefs, and conjectures regarding these existential topics. Many well-known philosophers seem to think they have it all figured out, yet questions remain open ended. Believe me, it is not my goal to explain everything. If it were, I would suggest that you put this book down and open another one, because this one would be a waste of your time. No one can explain everything. Not *life*, not *truth*, and certainly not *why*.

Chaos and confusion in the world—not only globally and politically, but in the lives of individuals and families—cause many sighs of sadness and perplexing questions. People often find that their hopes, dreams, plans, and expectations of a happy, fun, fulfilling life are dashed and destroyed, leaving them wondering what went wrong and why.

Why do these things happen? Why is there heartache, disappointment, pain, and trouble? Is it just cruel fate singling out people for failure and misery?

So as not to spend too much time laying a long-winded foundation for the main message of this book, let me get right to it.

Several years ago, as I was pondering questions regarding how and why things work the way they do, I was reading the book of Proverbs when a couple of verses seemed to highlight themselves in a way that caused me to pause and consider them anew. These are the verses:

INTRODUCTION

> The LORD by wisdom hath founded the earth; by understanding hath he established the heavens. By his knowledge the depths are broken up, and the clouds drop down the dew.
>
> Proverbs 3:19—20

(Because of the importance of these verses as pertaining to this book, they will be repeated several times in chapters to come.)

These verses were like a revelation to me. They seemed to declare that creation was not just the magical appearance of a physical, chaotic, unstructured world, but that it was all intricately designed with the knowledge, understanding, and wisdom of God. My conclusion was that creation not only *appeared* the way it did, but that it *functions* the way it does based upon these attributes of God's will; that is, his wisdom, understanding, and knowledge.

With that fresh understanding, many things began to make more sense to me. It seemed to say that the world works in the very way God designed it to work. As pertaining to us human beings, we are endowed with a certain nature that, even though we may differ from one another in a million ways, we all share an important commonality that we refer to as *human nature*. Of all the things about ourselves that we may be able to change, we cannot change that.

So, again, why do things work the way they do? Very simply, they work the way they do because that is the way God designed them to work. As we go along, I will refer to this as *creation law, the law of God*, or some variation of those phrases. (To be clear, this is not to be confused with the law of Moses or Old Testament law.)

Some of the issues I want to examine are:

- What relationship does the spiritual world have with the natural world?
- How can we know and understand how life works?
- Are our natural life and spiritual life intermingled, or are they totally separate and unrelated?
- Can we know how the things we do in the natural sense affect our spiritual life?
- What is the basis of the inner conflicts that we all experience?
- What can we learn from the fact that mankind is made in the image of God?
- What is the image of God?
- How is the make-up of man to be understood in the context of God's image?

These questions as well as others are examined in this book. I do not consider myself to be the arbiter of all that is true, nor do I claim to understand all the mysteries listed above. I do believe, however, that I have discovered, at least for myself, some very simple yet profound answers to many of these questions.

God not only created everything to *appear* in a certain way, but he designed his entire creation to *work* in a certain way as well. When we learn the way it works, we are more able to order our lives in the way that creates a flow of the blessings of God.

INTRODUCTION

ONE POINT OF CAUTION

Some readers might remember that back in the 1970s, several cultic, mystical, religious groups arose whose teachings and practices purported to usher adherents into a wonderful new existence of love, peace, and tranquility. Enlightenment was one of the terms used to describe the transformation people would experience when they implemented the teachings and entered what was claimed to be a new spiritual dimension. It was referred to as the "New Age" movement.

Without delving into a further description of this phenomenon, I want to assure you that this is *NOT* what this book is. I have no intention of offering some magical, mystical method of ensuring a life of health, wealth, luxury, and convenience. I will not promise that your humanity will be set aside in favor of some fairy tale existence. Although we have many biblical examples of God's people being immensely blessed, protected, and provided for, we have no examples of them living life with no problems, no hardships, and no challenges. We live, just as they did, in a fallen world. Even if we ourselves attempt to live our lives in accordance with the wisdom of God and the teaching of his word, not everyone else will. Because of this, we have to deal with what others do as well as what we do.

It is not my purpose to present a step-by-step, do-it-yourself plan for a successful life. My message will be more reminiscent of King David's prayer: "Shew me thy ways, O Lord; teach me thy paths" (Psalm 25:4).

THAT SAID...

In the chapters that follow, I hope to present in a concise, logical, convincing manner some of the answers I have discovered regarding how life works and how we can utilize this knowledge to live a truly blessed life. Hence, my subject:

"THAT'S JUST THE WAY IT WORKS"

This title is not intended to be an "in your face" declaration like *get used to it* or *deal with it*. In my view, "that's just the way it works" is a fitting answer to many questions we all have.

It is my hope that as you continue through this book, you will find some clarity regarding some of the issues you wonder about.

~ Chapter 1 ~

THE WISDOM OF SOLOMON

> *The LORD by wisdom hath founded the earth;*
> *by understanding hath he established the heavens.*
> *By his knowledge the depths are broken up,*
> *and the clouds drop down the dew.*
> *Proverbs 3:19–20*

Solomon was a remarkable man. Two of the most-read books of the Old Testament, Proverbs and Ecclesiastes, were, for the most part, written by him. The main focus of his writings was life and the wisdom he derived from living it. Much can be learned not only from Solomon's writings, but from his life as well.

The verses above are the starting point of what this book is about. They arrested my attention a few years ago and ultimately became the basis for what you will be reading in this book.

To give context to all that will be said regarding these words in the books of Proverbs and Ecclesiastes, let's take a brief look at Solomon's story.

THE WISDOM OF SOLOMON—WHERE DID IT COME FROM?

Was Solomon just a really smart guy, or what? He is, of course, regarded by many as the wisest man that ever lived other than Jesus Christ. But why?

The story that relates how and why Solomon acquired such amazing wisdom is quite interesting. It begins with King Saul and his successor, King David, Solomon's father. Let's take a very brief look at the history that led to Solomon becoming king.

THE SITUATION

Many years before Solomon was even born, a man named Samuel, a prophet of God, judged Israel. This simply means he was Israel's leader. When Samuel grew old, he installed his sons into leadership positions as was the custom in Israel. Unfortunately, Samuel's sons were not godly men like their father, so the elders of Israel came to Samuel asking him to consider giving them a king. Other nations had kings, they said, and they wanted to be like the other nations.

Samuel was deeply offended by this request and went to God with his complaint. He told God that he felt rejected by the people he had served faithfully for so many years. God's response to Samuel was that the people had not rejected him as their leader; they had rejected God.

God told Samuel to go ahead and consider the people's request, but he was to tell them how different life would be for them with a king. A king would require much of the people: their sons and daughters would be drafted into the king's service; their lands and livestock would be taken from them for the king's use; they would be required to pay exorbitant taxes. The people, however, had made up their minds. They wanted a king. So God told Samuel to give them what they wanted.

The first man chosen to be this new king was Saul. We can infer from the biblical description that Saul was quite handsome. I'm not sure how bright he was, but he certainly had the looks.

Things didn't work out all that well with Saul. He didn't seem to grasp the fact that even though he was the king, he was still expected to obey God. Because of a blatant act of rebellion, God took the kingdom from Saul, stating that it would be given to another.

Whom would God choose to succeed Saul? Samuel was about to find out. The Lord instructed him to go to Bethlehem to the house of Jesse where he would find among Jesse's sons the one who was to be the next king. Assuming that one of Jesse's three elder sons would be chosen, Samuel considered each one, expecting God to make his choice known. After a procession of sons had been presented, Samuel realized that none of them would be chosen and asked Jesse if there were any others. Yes, Jesse said, while indicating that he was just a young shepherd boy and certainly not a logical choice to be king. When David was brought before Samuel, God made it known that the lad would be the next king and that Samuel was to anoint him there and then. So in a private family ceremony Samuel anointed a young shepherd boy named David as the new king of Israel.

David was a special person in many ways. In fact, Samuel told Saul that the Lord had chosen David because he was a man after God's own heart.

Now this transition didn't take place immediately. In fact, it was several years before David finally occupied the throne of Israel. The interim between the time David was anointed king by Samuel and the time he ultimately began to reign was long and tumultuous not only for David, but for Israel as well. Saul did not go quietly; he clung tenaciously to his position while trying desperately to kill his young replacement.

The event that sealed David's fate as Saul's hated nemesis was the killing of the Philistine giant Goliath. David, the only one in all of Israel who was brave enough to respond to the challenges of this giant warrior, established himself as the darling of the nation. It did not sit well with Saul when he heard the throngs of Israel's women chanting, "Saul hath slain his thousands, and David his ten thousands" (1 Samuel 18:7).

David, a man highly revered in scripture, was not without his own personal failings. The most egregious example of David's sins was his affair with Bathsheba followed by his efforts to cover it up. Bathsheba was a beautiful woman who happened to be the wife of Uriah, a trustworthy officer in David's army. During the time of one of Israel's wars, David sent his troops out to fight the battle while he enjoyed the comforts of the palace. That was when he caught sight of Bathsheba and sent for her. As a result of this ill-contrived tryst, Bathsheba became pregnant. When she informed David, he sent word to Joab, his general, to send Uriah home, hoping he would spend a couple of days with his wife. This, David thought, would give him cover for the sin he had committed. Bathsheba would have her child, and everyone, including Uriah, would assume that Uriah was the father.

To David's dismay, Uriah was too loyal to his fellow warriors who were still on the battlefield. He felt it would be unfair to those who were in the heat of the battle, away from their families, risking their lives for him to enjoy a vacation with his wife, so he simply refused to go home. He chose instead to camp out on the palace steps.

When Plan A failed, David had to institute Plan B. He drafted a letter to Joab, instructing him to put Uriah in a strategic position on the front lines where he would surely be killed, going so far as to send the sealed instructions back to Joab by Uriah's hand. Shortly after that, Uriah was dead.

Soon after the child was born, the prophet Nathan confronted David with his terrible sin, at which point David sincerely repented. The damage, however, was done. A short time later the child died, leaving David in emotional shambles.

Eventually, Bathsheba, who had become David's wife, gave birth to Solomon.

As David lay dying, one of his other sons, Adonijah, plotted to take the throne by force even though David had promised that Solomon, not Adonijah, would be his successor. A fierce battle ensued during which time Adonijah tried to seize the throne. David, however, being informed of the attempted coup, reiterated his declaration that Solomon was to be king and not Adonijah. So, in a quickly arranged ceremony, Solomon was anointed by the priest and the prophet and with great fanfare was declared the new king of Israel.

Even though David would always be considered Israel's greatest king, his family was a mess (e.g., murder, rebellion, evil intrigue), and the kingdom was not much better. Thus it was into this volatile environment that Solomon was thrust as the new king of Israel.

THE DREAM

One night in a dream, the Lord appeared to Solomon with an amazing offer. The King James Version records it like this:

> *In Gibeon the* LORD *appeared to Solomon in a dream by night: and God said, Ask what I shall give thee.*
> 1 Kings 3:5

This looks like a blank check signed by the Lord himself. If that offer were extended to me, I'm not sure what I would say. Hopefully, I would respond as thoughtfully as Solomon did and ask self*less*ly rather than self*ish*ly. But I digress.

What was Solomon's answer? The King James Version renders it like this:

> *And Solomon said, Thou hast shewed unto thy servant David my father great mercy, according as he walked before thee in truth, and in righteousness, and in uprightness of heart with thee; and thou hast kept for him this great kindness, that thou hast given him a son to sit on his throne, as it is this day. And now, O Lord my God, thou hast made thy servant king instead of David my father: and I am but a little child: I know not how to go out or come in. And thy servant is in the midst of thy people which thou hast chosen, a great people, that cannot be numbered nor counted for multitude. Give therefore thy servant an understanding heart to judge thy people, that I may discern between good and bad: for who is able to judge this thy so great a people?*
>
> 1 Kings 3:6–9

Not everyone reads the King James Version of the Bible these days, so let me just give a few words of clarification.

Solomon must have been a bit overwhelmed regarding his new responsibilities as king of Israel, especially considering the chaos and confusion that prevailed at the time. It was as if Solomon was saying, *I have no clue what to do here, Lord. Please help me out. I need* some wisdom to know how to handle this new role. When I think of all I have to deal with, I feel like a little kid. These are your people, and I have to provide leadership to them. They deserve someone who knows what he's doing, so if you could just give me a wise and understanding heart, I would really appreciate it.

That request impressed the Lord, so let's see how the King James Version renders God's amazing response:

> *And the speech pleased the Lord, that Solomon had asked this thing. And God said unto him, Because thou hast asked this thing, and hast not asked for thyself long life; neither hast asked riches for thyself, nor hast asked the life of thine enemies; but hast asked for thyself understanding to discern judgment; Behold, I have done according to thy words: lo, I have given thee a wise and an understanding heart; so that there was none like thee before thee, neither after thee shall any arise like unto thee.*
>
> 1 Kings 3:10–12

Okay, that's rather simple. The Lord said that Solomon could have asked for anything—long life, lots of money, or even the destruction of all his enemies. Obviously, he didn't ask for any of those things, so, God gave him exactly what he did ask for—wisdom.

If you read on, though, you will find that not only did the Lord grant wisdom unto Solomon, but he also gave him all the things for which he could have asked but didn't.

This amazing response shows the nature of the wonderful God that we serve. He not only gives us what we need but often gives us much more.

SO WHAT DOES ALL THIS MEAN?

God gave Solomon immediate wisdom beyond his age and experience, and it didn't take long for that wisdom to be called upon when the famous dilemma regarding the two women and two babies was presented to him.

The women were prostitutes who shared the same house. Each one had an infant son. One night one of the women rolled over on her son and suffocated him. When she realized what had happened, she panicked. Quickly and quietly, she exchanged the babies, putting her dead son in bed with the other woman and the living child in her own bed. When the other woman discovered the dead baby in her bed, she knew it was not her son and quickly realized what had been done.

The two women took their predicament to King Solomon, each declaring that the living son was hers and wanting the king to rule accordingly. Of course, Solomon had no way of knowing which woman was telling the truth, so he called for a sword. "Divide the living child in two, and give half to the one, and half to the other," Solomon decreed, (1 Kings 3:25).

Immediately, the rightful mother spoke up, asking that the child's life be spared and given to the other woman. Solomon then knew this woman was indeed the true mother because she was willing to give up her son rather than see him die. The real mother was awarded her son.

Reports of this incident were soon heard by all of Israel and there was immediate respect for Solomon. Everyone recognized that the wisdom of God was in him.

~ Chapter 2 ~
THE POWER OF OBSERVATION

Throughout many years of preaching, teaching, studying, and observing life, I have come to see the book of Proverbs differently from how I saw it in my youth. Although I truly consider it to be divinely inspired just as the rest of the Bible is, I don't particularly see it as a book of absolutes. Please don't misunderstand— I believe everything in the Bible is *absolutely* true; it's just that Proverbs is true in the context of what a proverb is. That is, the proverbs are general truths. They are not necessarily absolutes. One might say that a proverb is a "rule of thumb," a short statement regarding something that has been observed by a wise person—in this case, Solomon.

Once again, let me remind you that my intent regarding this book is not to delve into the original Greek and Hebrew texts to explain the book of Proverbs and create a new theological work. My hope is to provide a very practical, down-to-earth presentation regarding what Solomon's wisdom as found in his proverbs means for all of us.

SOLOMON, AN INTENSE OBSERVER OF LIFE

Solomon, by virtue of God's gift to him, became an intense observer of life. He wanted to know how it all worked. He wanted to be able to glean from his own personal experiences as well as the experiences of others to give concise statements of general truth. It was as though he was saying, *Although the possible number of variables is infinite, this is generally how it all works.* God gave him a unique ability to categorize all that he saw of life situations and derive from his experiences concise proverbs to provide wisdom for those who would read and learn.

It is my belief that Solomon discovered a foundational truth that goes beyond just a tutorial of dos and don'ts—rewards for doing the right things and punishments for doing the wrong things. It is something of a revelation to me that Solomon's wisdom was about how God created everything and how he specifically designed that creation to work the way it does.

In other words, Solomon was saying in essence (and this is very important), *This is the way it all works, and the reason it works this way is that God created it and ordained it to work this way.*

Solomon's conclusions were more than simple deductions based solely upon his keen observation skills. They were, I believe, the result of divine revelation regarding God's creation and how it all functions and why.

In my own ministry (and I'm aware I'm not Solomon), there were times when I made statements or predictions about how I expected certain things to turn out based upon what I saw people doing. Occasionally someone, after hearing my conclusions, would mildly challenge me, saying, *Well, how do you know?* Very often my answer would be, *That's just the way it works,* which is precisely where the title of this book came from.

OBSERVING WISDOM IN THE STREETS

As we consider the importance of observation in one's personal accumulation of wisdom, let's look at the first chapter of Proverbs.

It is the first time wisdom speaks to us as if it were a person, and it is personified as a woman. Look at how *she* is introduced.

> *Wisdom crieth without; she uttereth her voice in the streets: she crieth in the chief place of concourse, in the openings of the gates: in the city she uttereth her words.*
> *Proverbs 1:20–21*

This tells us that wisdom is not something available *only* in the Bible. There is plenty to be learned about how things work simply by observing life around us. As it says in the verses above, wisdom speaks even in the streets. We can learn a lot simply by observation.

Let me offer one brief example, a familiar observation presented by Solomon.

> *A soft answer turns away wrath, but a harsh word stirs up anger.*
> *Proverbs 15:1, NKJV*

What happens when you speak cheerfully, kindly, and respectfully to your spouse, your children, your friends, or your coworkers as opposed to when you speak harshly or critically? I think we all know the answer.

This is just one simple example of what we are discussing. One need not read the Bible to know this. Just be an observer.

Wisdom tells us that much of the quality of our relationships depends on what *we* do, not what is done to us.

We will speak more of this woman, Wisdom, later.

KNOWLEDGE, UNDERSTANDING, AND WISDOM

Where did everything come from? By *everything*, I mean *everything*—all matter. Was there a beginning to it all, or has it just always been? Is there any rhyme or reason in creation, or was there just some giant explosion of matter a few billion years ago and this is the result? Is it all just happenstance, or is there some form of intelligence behind it all?

A Brief Pause for a Personal Opinion

Questions have arisen about the "Big Bang Theory." If one accepts the validity of that theory, then where did exploding matter that formed the universe come from? Some scientists would have us believe it had no beginning; it always has just been. My extremely limited knowledge of physics makes it impossible for me to grasp the theories that would explain such an assumption.

Here is my amazingly simple theory. I say "theory" because that is all it is. I cannot prove any assumption that I have about creation any more than anyone else can prove their assumption. My belief, however, is that there was no universe, no space, no physical matter until God spoke it into existence. How long ago was that? I do not know. Neither does anyone else.

AS I WAS SAYING ...

As previously mentioned, in reading the book of Proverbs some time ago, two verses caught my attention and spoke to me in a specific way, helping me to understand some things I had always wondered about. It was, for me, the beginning of the coming together of many pieces to an exceptionally large puzzle. From that point many things began to make more sense to me. Though it may seem repetitive, I would like to present these verses once again, since they are essential to the main message of this book.

> The LORD by wisdom hath founded the earth; by understanding hath he established the heavens. By his knowledge the depths are broken up, and the clouds drop down the dew.
>
> *Proverbs 3:19–20*

Some may view these verses as a lofty, poetic account regarding God's creation, designed simply to inspire awe and not to be taken literally.

In my view, these verses tell us that the very fabric of creation is literally interwoven with the wisdom, understanding, and knowledge of God.

Rephrased, the statement means all of God's creation is founded upon and operates in accordance with his wisdom, understanding, and knowledge. (From this point and for the sake of readability, when I refer to God's wisdom, it also will include his understanding and knowledge. In him they all are one.)

Some assume that God just flung everything out into the universe to find its own way to function, but I believe the truth to be that it all functions on the principles God created the universe by. God did nothing haphazardly; he had a distinct purpose for everything he created. Everything works the way it does because God ordained it to work that way. The more I understand about that, the more efficiently I can order my life.

A Brief Pause for Further Explanation

What do the verses in Proverbs 3:19–20 tell us? They explain in layers the divine plan for the entire creation. Let's look at each part.

The Lord by wisdom hath founded the earth. This means that God's wisdom was the very foundation for the earth itself.

By understanding, hath he established the heavens. The functions of the heavens, the atmosphere, the universe, including the sun, moon, stars and all the galaxies, are established by God's understanding.

By his knowledge the depths are broken up, and the clouds drop down the dew. The inner workings of planet Earth, the fountains of the deep, and even the clouds above are governed by the knowledge of God. It all functions in accordance with his will simply because he created it to do so.

These verses form the foundation for the conclusions I am attempting to explain in this book, so yes, they are very important. They are not, however, stand-alone verses. Several other writers convey similar explanations of how God's wisdom was incorporated into the creation. Here are a few examples:

> *O Lord, how manifold are thy works! in wisdom hast thou made them all: the earth is full of thy riches.*
> *Psalm 104:24*

> *To him that by wisdom made the heavens: for his mercy endureth for ever. To him that stretched out the earth above the waters: for his mercy endureth for ever. To him that made great lights: for his mercy endureth for ever: The sun to rule by day: for his mercy endureth*

for ever: The moon and stars to rule by night: for his mercy endureth for ever.

Psalm 136:5–9

When he prepared the heavens, I [Wisdom] was there: when he set a compass upon the face of the depth: When he established the clouds above: when he strengthened the fountains of the deep: When he gave to the sea his decree, that the waters should not pass his commandment: when he appointed the foundations of the earth.

Proverbs 8:27–29

He hath made the earth by his power, he hath established the world by his wisdom, and hath stretched out the heavens by his discretion. When he uttereth his voice, there is a multitude of waters in the heavens, and he causeth the vapours to ascend from the ends of the earth; he maketh lightnings with rain, and bringeth forth the wind out of his treasures.

Jeremiah 10:12–13

The point is that what we read in the verses cited in Proverbs 3 are explanations about the creation and how God's wisdom is the basis, not only for its existence, but its function. It stands to reason that all of God's creation is permeated with this same wisdom. All plant life, animal life, and even human life was established upon the same creative principles. We call it nature.

BACK TO THE SUBJECT OF OBSERVATION

My advice is to read the Bible and study the book of Proverbs, but also keep your eyes and ears open. Hear what people say, know what they believe, see what they do, and observe the results of their choices. You may learn some valuable lessons that will help you to make good decisions that result in good outcomes and avoid some of the negative results of poor decisions in your own life.

~ Chapter 3 ~
HOW I BECAME AN OBSERVER

(A Brief Personal Story)

The view into my background presented in this chapter may provide some context to my way of thinking and offer insight into how I came to many of the conclusions set forth in this book. It may help to make better sense about what I think and the rationale behind it.

I view Solomon as a serious and analytical observer of life. His amazing wisdom, a gift from God, enabled him to process all he saw in such a way as to draw insightful conclusions worthy of being preserved through the ages. The books of Proverbs and Ecclesiastes are the result.

Now I'm no Solomon. However, I am an observer of life. What follows is a bit of background that may explain why I view myself in that way.

A BIT DYSFUNCTIONAL? MAYBE

Growing up, my family could have been considered somewhat dysfunctional. The situation never felt as chaotic to me as some may have thought it to be. To me it was just life. My parents divorced when I was six years old, so for the next several years my sister and I lived with several different combinations of family members and a few kind friends. This necessitated a lot of moving—emphasis on *a lot*. I changed schools close to twenty times before graduating from high school. Some years I attended two different schools, and at least two years I attended three.

As one might imagine, I tended to be rather detached. Always being the new kid was not easy, and my way of dealing with that was to avoid trying to insert myself quickly into any social circles. I was quite wary of saying or doing anything that would draw the wrong kind of attention to myself. I've often said that while waiting for the first bell to ring signaling the start of class time, I tried my best to look like a locker—you know, to blend in with the scenery so as not to be noticed. Kids who had attended the same schools for years with each other could be cruel to the newcomer. At least that was my assumption, so my way of dealing with that was to make sure I did nothing stupid. Unfortunately, that tended to mean I didn't do anything at all beyond what was absolutely necessary. This could partially explain why education was not high on my list of priorities as a young person. I was just trying to do what I could to survive in unfamiliar environments.

I was not a great student in school. Even though I got mostly A's and B's and an occasional C, I never really challenged myself with classes that would tax my brain. I did graduate from high school and actually made it into the upper third of my class, but I got there mostly by taking the easiest classes. Given the choice of pursuing the "academic" or the "general" course of study, as they were tagged in my school, I chose "general." No advanced classes for me. Not that I thought I wasn't smart enough, but mostly because college prep classes seemed almost foreign to me. Also, I think that on some level I chose to be in classes where I knew I would do well rather than where I thought I may struggle. Besides, college prep classes were for those who were headed for college. Me? Why should I think that I would ever go to college?

My family was just not into education. As far as I know, I was one of the first of my family on my father's side to even graduate from high school. Education was not a high priority among many of my aunts and uncles in those days. Thankfully, things have changed and many of my cousins and their sons and daughters are highly educated and have done very well in life.

THREE MEMORABLE SCHOOL EXPERIENCES

Looking back, I recall some interesting experiences that stamped lasting impressions on my mind, the cumulative effect of which resulted in the theme of this book. Hence, the title *That's Just the Way It Works*.

Even in the most difficult of environments, life has a way of incorporating notable, life-altering experiences. While some of those experiences are amazing, others are just ordinary moments that for some reason stay with you, even to the point of helping to mold your life. Here are three of those experiences I still remember quite vividly.

THANKS, MR. CAM

As a ninth grader I had a science class in which I received a B or C (I don't recall which). I remember my teacher's name, and I remember really liking him. He had a great vocabulary and spoke rather eloquently, which really impressed me. I still remember what this teacher wrote in the area of my report card designated "Teacher's Comments." He stated, "Ron can do better; however, he seems content to remain in the status quo." It was signed "CAM." That stings now, and I guess it stung then because it is still vivid in my memory.

A MUCH-NEEDED CHALLENGE

It was my junior year of high school in Crawfordsville, Indiana. My English teacher was a very attractive young woman whom I remember as Ms. S. The class was just basic English and I was doing well, getting a solid A. One day Ms. S stopped me on my way out of class, wanting to talk to me. She said something like this: "Ron, I really enjoy having you in my class and you are doing very well, but it is my opinion that you don't really belong in this class. If you don't mind, I'm going to recommend that you be placed in Advanced English. You don't have to change if you don't want to, but I think it would be best for you."

To be honest, I don't remember what I thought at the time. I don't recall feeling flattered; it just seemed that someone who apparently cared about me and knew better than I, thought I should make the change. So who was I to disagree? A couple days later I was in Advanced English, a little bit behind, but actually energized and excited to be there.

Sitting next to me was a nice girl named Cindy. She was one of those popular few who knew everyone and was very well liked by all our classmates. She was friendly and welcomed me to the class. It made me feel as though I actually belonged, and even though I had to study harder, being in that class was a very positive experience for me.

THIS IS JUST HOW IT WORKED FOR ME

I also took a class in accounting at Crawfordsville High School. Mr. RM was the teacher. His requirement for us at the beginning of the class was to memorize what the correct balance of each kind of account was—debit or credit. I think there were six types of accounts, but it's been over fifty years, so don't hold me to that. Mr. RM wanted us to be able to immediately tell him what the correct balance was as soon as he mentioned the type of account. That required what I would call rote memorization, and I wasn't good at it. I tried to learn it that way, but after the first grading period, I had a C. Although I was not as dedicated to my studies as I should have been, I hated C's.

How it happened I don't know, but eventually I began to understand *why* the balances were what they were, and from that point it all began to make sense to me. When Mr. RM mentioned an account, it would take me a few seconds to think about it, but I always could give the correct answer. From that time, the entire subject was very easy for me. Accounting is all about logic and all the balances must agree, so as soon as I understood the basics, I was able to understand everything that would be added throughout the year. It all just made sense. The result was straight A's the rest of the year. In fact, after one particular test when nearly everyone in the class failed, I ended up with a grade of 100 percent. Mr. RM had me stand up and try to teach the class. Whether or not that helped was never clear, but I still remember the incident.

If you're thinking, *This guy is quite the braggart*, please set that assumption aside. That was the only class in which I was able to achieve that level of success. In all the rest, I was just there like everyone else.

OKAY, HERE'S ONE MORE

It may seem odd that I would mention this experience, but it emphasizes the positive effect we can have on others when we are nice enough to notice them.

I don't even remember the particular class, but it was at Crawfordsville High School. It was most likely my senior year, and the teacher was an "elderly" woman—you know, fiftyish. (My, how perceptions change!) The class was over and we were walking out of the room. I was wearing a royal blue sweater that had a ten-inch zipper that started in the middle of my chest and extended up to the collar. The teacher stopped me and commented, "Ron, you should wear blue all the time. You look so nice in that blue sweater." I have no idea how I responded, but I certainly remember the comment. She simply said something nice and complimentary to me. It made me feel good. Come to think of it, I do wear blue a lot.

Most of my life growing up, I usually had two pairs of pants and two shirts to wear to school. I tried to make sure they were interchangeable color wise so it looked like I had more clothes than I actually did. Positive comments like that nice teacher gave me were memorable.

God created us to be nice to one another, to have positive effects on those around us. Things like that didn't give me "the big head"; they just made me feel better about myself and about those who showed they cared about me.

That's just the way it works.

SO THREE OR FOUR EXPERIENCES—BIG DEAL

My upbringing was not horrible, although I could tell it in such a way as to make it seem horrible. I'm just not into sad stories that make people feel sorry for me. I don't feel sorry for myself, and I don't want anyone else to either. As I said before, to me it was just life.

That said, there were plenty of negatives my sister and I had to deal with. The great thing is that there were some wonderful positives too. To this day, I have no ill feelings toward my mother or my father despite what some conventional wisdom would expect. I dearly loved them both. I never had to get over any bitterness against them because I never had any.

It is my contention that we either can focus on all the negatives and play the part of a victim, or we can see the good things that happened along the way that gave us reason to know that everything would be all right.

I won't take time to list the many good people who came across my path during my growing up years who inspired me, but I want to explain why I chose the experiences above to illustrate how I have come to believe what I believe about how things work.

HERE GOES . . .

My ninth-grade science teacher, Mr. CAM, chided me by saying I was "content to remain in the status quo." In so doing, he made me realize that one can just coast and get by or expend a bit more effort and more fully realize one's potential. Success is reserved for those who will go beyond the minimum requirement and do the "extra credit." *That's just the way it works.*

My English teacher, Ms. S, reinforced what Mr. CAM said, only she didn't write it in a comment on my report card. Instead, she gently pushed me beyond my comfort zone into a more rewarding area of endeavor. One can, as so many do, languish in the comfort zone of little effort and get by, but there is much greater satisfaction in working a little harder and doing a little better. *That's just the way it works.*

Mr. RM allowed me to learn in the very best way that I could. Once he realized how I learned best, he continued to guide me and encourage me. Thanks to him, I was able to actually be the very best in something, at least among his classes. Up to that time, I had been satisfied to be mediocre when I didn't always have to be.

In Mr. RM's accounting class, I learned that if I could understand how something works, I could build upon that understanding. That's the reason I'm excited about the discovery God has allowed me to have about life and how it works and why. That's also the reason I decided to try to write a book about it.

I see many things clearly now that once were kind of hazy. For most of my life, I saw "the rules" as being somewhat arbitrary and maybe a little disjointed. I tried to follow those rules the best I could, but I did so simply because I saw obedience as a very important principle. Please don't misunderstand. Obedience really *is* an important principle. But when we seek to follow rules that seem arbitrary or random, we can struggle and eventually go astray. When we realize that God's laws are not arbitrary but are based upon the way God created life to work, we can see that living by God's laws produces great results in our lives. It creates a flow of blessing in us and through us.

The wisdom of God and his word teaches us more than just one alternative way of living. It is a revelation of how and why the world works as it does. The more we read God's word and observe life as it happens around us, the more we realize God's revelation to us concerning it.

That's just the way it works.

A BRIEF DISCLAIMER

When I write about people making the choices that ultimately control their destiny, I may use my own self as an example of someone who chose not to go down the path that had seemingly been forged before me by my somewhat dysfunctional upbringing. However, I must add that along with whatever negative examples I had, there also were some wonderful examples of a completely different kind of life.

When I was fourteen, I was privileged to spend nine months with a wonderful couple named Bill and Willie. They took me into their home and treated me like a son. (More than sixty years later they're still treating me like a son.) For those nine wonderful months, I was privileged to live in a home where there was no drinking, no arguing or fussing, and no threats of divorce. It was literally the next thing to heaven to me. It was then that I made a conscious decision that when I grew up and got married, I wanted to have a home like Bill and Willie had. When I had girlfriends, I always tried to bring them to Bill and Willie's house to see if they approved. (I didn't tell the girls that though.) When I married my wife, Julie, she had their overwhelming approval. Happily, she continues to have that approval to this day.

Another very important influence in my life was my pastor, JHY. Pastor Y was a cousin, but more than that, he was like a father to me. He seemed to believe in me, and that was a very important factor in my development as a young man. Pastor Y was one of my heroes from the time I was nine years old until now, even though he passed away many years ago.

Another man I would like to mention is NLH. He was my pastor during my last two years of high school. Pastor H and his family took my sister Judy and me under their wings and treated us like family. Our parents did not attend church at all and had no interest in seeing that we attended either. Every single week until I had my own car, Pastor H would drive out to the country where we lived and pick us up for church and take us home afterward. This was Sunday morning, Sunday night, and Wednesday night. When we had special revival services, he did it every night. When Pastor H's family fed the visiting ministers at their home following the services, Judy and I were almost always there. I cannot say enough good things about this family and how influential they were to my sister and me.

I said all of that to say that I realize many do not have the same mixture of positive and negative influences I had growing up. Some kids are surrounded by nothing but bad. As a result, that's all they know. They hardly have a chance. Our hearts should go out to those who are virtually forced into lives of drugs, sex, crime, anger, bitterness, and hatred.

As I write these words, I have no idea how many will ever read them, but it is my genuine hope that someone will read them and discover that there's a way that life can work very well, and if we align ourselves with those principles, we will reap the positive benefits that are available to anyone and everyone.

That's just the way it works.

ONE MORE THING

Writing this chapter about my life is certainly not for the purpose of comparing myself in any way to Solomon. Solomon is in a category all his own. The rest of us simply try to learn all we can by reading and studying his writings. The vast treasure of wisdom that he left is of immense value to all people. This chapter is more about how I came to think, reason, and at least attempt to understand life based upon my own experiences. My way of thinking and observing, I believe, provides the basis for my understanding of Solomon, his thinking process, and his wise conclusions.

As one might determine in reading this chapter, I was usually an outsider. It may even sound as if I was a recluse, that I lived in my own world inside a shell. That was not the case. I was just very careful, more of an observer than a participant. Thus my hesitancy to insert myself into the social structure of a new school was a symptom of trying to figure out whether I could find common ground between myself and others.

I watched how the others interacted with one another, how friendly they seemed, whether there were hard and fast cliques that were maintained, or whether there seemed to be any evidence of openness among them. As a result, I think I learned a lot about people.

It is difficult for anyone to be vastly different from how he or she was raised. While I was never fearful of people, I was always careful. This tendency carried over somewhat into my adult life, not to the point of dysfunction, as I've always had lots of friends. But I've always been an observer.

TOO MUCH INFORMATION?
I WONDERED THAT TOO

Several friends and family members told me that people like personal stories, so now you know mine. I hope it helps.

~ Chapter 4 ~
LIFE IS HARD

Man that is born of a woman is of few days, and full of trouble.
Job 14:1

YES, LIFE *IS* HARD

What a wonderful, positive, encouraging statement to open a new chapter, right? As is often the case, a contextual understanding of the statement is necessary.

The verse above from the book of Job may sound like the ultimate expression of pessimism, negativism, and cynicism, but I don't think that is the intended message. The actual message is that life is filled with uncertainty and, along with the many good things we have or encounter, there are difficult things that come along as well. Sometimes they come without warning and for no apparent reason.

With that in mind, I hope you will bear with me for just a few paragraphs while I attempt to place this "life is hard" statement in context.

Several years ago, I was sitting in a fast-food restaurant with a long-time friend of mine for whom I have always had the highest regard. We were discussing some family issues that were common to most of us. This man, typically a very positive person who rarely described anything with a negative spin, described some of the challenges his children were experiencing, none of which were that different from those experienced by others. During this conversation, he surprised me by saying that *life is hard*. I guess I remembered his words because I was surprised that he would express it that way.

What he meant was simply this: life can be very complicated in terms of choices, opportunities, and decisions regarding how we are going to live our lives. People are raised a certain way, but when they launch out on their own, they must determine whether they are going to live as their parents taught them or opt for one of countless other ways.

When children are raised by Christian parents, they are taught various principles that often differ greatly from how other people live. They may feel they were restricted in ways that are difficult to maintain even if they wanted to, and often they don't really want to.

They are bombarded with many other philosophies that counter what they were taught. Being free of parental oversight, they make many decisions based on what's "cool" or "in." The desire to be accepted and liked by their peers lures many of them into lifestyles that were never acceptable at home.

As the young person weighs all the options, choices are often made that result in unforeseen and certainly unintended consequences.

Life is hard because there are so many options and so little understanding of what those options eventually produce in the life of the person making the choices.

MAKING SENSE OF A HARD LIFE

Everyone has a story, and each one is filled with a mixture of good times and bad, triumph and tragedy, laughter and tears. No one's life is all good and no one's is all bad, but regardless of who we are, we can all be faced with the realization that life can at times be hard.

Regardless of the circumstances that come our way, our lives are ultimately the result of the choices we make. With few exceptions, no one is forced to walk a particular path. We can be guided by good influences or by bad influences.

Admittedly, some negative environmental situations can be overwhelming, and when some people end up doing bad things, others, considering their background, might say, *Oh, well, just look at how they were raised. It's no surprise.*

It's true. Most people tend to be what they are taught to be, go where they are led, and act the way they see people around them act. It's hard to forge a path different from the ones our families and friends have walked. We know what we are taught; we do what we know; we experience whatever consequences that follow. Unfortunately, we don't always see the correlation between bad consequences and the actions that produced them.

The reason? Things work the way they work, and there's really no escaping it. The more we understand life itself and how it works, the better able we are to make intelligent choices regarding how we live.

I believe God has given us access through his word to the teaching that will enable us to better understand life. I'm afraid, though, that most people decide that if they do whatever is convenient or popular or mainstream, everything will work out. If it doesn't, it's just a quirk of fate—just one of those things.

ABOUT THAT "LIFE IS HARD" THING

Let's be honest. Life is filled with challenges. Even when we're trying to do the right things, there are those around us who are not. No one can control what others do, and we do not individually create all the circumstances we end up having to deal with. All of us together affect each other's lives by what we do. Sometimes we may get frustrated at having to deal with problems we didn't cause but find ourselves stuck with anyway.

As I continue to write this book, I have no illusions of being able to convince anyone that if they do as I say, all of their problems will be eliminated. That's NOT the way it works.

So, even though life can be hard (sometimes extremely hard!), God has given us through the wisdom of his word instruction that can help us to generate a flow of blessing through our lives, blessing for us as well as for those around us. It is by this wisdom that we can learn to cope with difficult times and situations.

ONE MORE THING (Speaking as a Pastor)

Before I move on from this "Life Is Hard" chapter, let me add one more thought. It occurs to me that someone could be reading this who is experiencing excruciating pain, whether physical, mental, or emotional. It may sound as though your situation is being minimized by the idea that life and all the good and bad that occurs is simply about choices.

You may rightfully ask yourself, or me if you had the chance, *What choices did I make that have landed me in this horrible place? As far as I know, I have always made or tried to make good choices. I have loved and served the Lord the best I know how. What I am going through doesn't seem to be the result or the consequence of my poor choices. It just seems to have come out of the blue and I don't understand.*

I have no desire to present some oversimplified notion that if I just do all the right things, I will create my own little primrose path of pleasure, health, wealth, and convenience. Life is filled with twists and turns that cannot be foreseen or controlled. I have the utmost sympathy for those who suffer without knowing why. And believe me, it happens. (You may want to consider my observations about Job in chapters 14 and 16 of this book.)

What I am hoping to convey is simply that in our good times—and even in those awful times—the principles of God are always right. They will always produce better results than the alternatives. Always.

So my prayers are for all who are reading these words even during confusing, painful circumstances. I do know that God loves you and will continue to strengthen you even in your hard times.

Please try not to forget that.

~ Chapter 5 ~

KNOWLEDGE, UNDERSTANDING, AND WISDOM

This book is not just a study of the book of Proverbs; it is a study of how things work—how life works. One might say it is a philosophy of life in accordance with Bible teaching.

It appears that Solomon realized a foundational truth regarding creation. Genesis 1:1 states, "In the beginning God created the heaven and the earth." It is my opinion that all of God's creation—both physical and spiritual—is established on the same principles. In other words, both the spiritual world *and* the physical world are founded on the wisdom of God.

Obviously, the spiritual world already existed when the physical world was created, and yet the physical world virtually mirrors the spiritual world, being established on the same foundation of the knowledge, understanding, and wisdom of God.

To help me explain what I mean by this, let's look once more at our text in Proverbs.

> *The LORD by wisdom hath founded the earth; by understanding hath he established the heavens. By his knowledge the depths are broken up, and the clouds drop down the dew.*
>
> *Proverbs 3:19–20*

The conclusion I draw from these verses is simple. Not only did God create the earth and everything else by his wisdom, understanding, and knowledge, but all of God's creation is founded upon these divine attributes.

God's wisdom is indeed the foundation for all that he created. And not just the foundation itself, mind you, but everything that is established upon that foundation.

I realize I've said this before, but I would like to say it once again: The fabric of all of God's creation is interwoven with God's wisdom. This metaphor, I think, helps to demonstrate the pervasiveness of these attributes throughout all that God set forth by his creative word. Not only did God use his wisdom to create everything, but the entire creation itself functions in accordance with the laws and principles of that wisdom. Everything God created operates just as his wisdom dictates.

THE CHOICES ARE OURS

Personally, I do not believe in predestination in terms of a person's final eternal reward. Further, I do not believe, as some theologians do, that God, by virtue of his sovereignty, dictates everything that happens down to the smallest detail. We all have a God-given freedom to make choices, and those choices set us on paths that have consequences. We all live in a system created by God, and that system works the same for everyone. It is based upon laws that govern many things in our lives.

Take the natural law of gravity, for example. You may not like it. You may, in fact, disagree with it, thinking it is a ridiculous law. But it is in force just the same. It cannot be altered, amended, or changed in any way. It is not subject to debate or vote. It cannot be appealed or repealed. It is an established law. So my advice is, regardless of what you think of the law of gravity, do not attempt to leap tall buildings in a single bound. If you do, you will undoubtedly break more than just a law.

There is no "punishment" for breaking the law of gravity. One simply experiences the natural consequences of his or her actions. This, in my view, is what happens to us in life. God has designed his creation to work in a certain way, and that way is explained in the Bible. When we align our lives with those laws, we experience the good results of our life choices. When we do not, we experience the negative results of our bad choices.

Solomon, in his writings, says God has established his creation to function in a certain way. It is as though, through Solomon and others, God is giving us an understanding of life. He is saying, *That's just the way it works.*

And this is true in both the physical and the spiritual realms.

KNOWLEDGE, UNDERSTANDING, AND WISDOM

These three aspects of intelligence seem to be used interchangeably in Proverbs. This may be because they are all resident in God and are not part of any developmental process. God is not learning. He is not gaining greater understanding as time goes by. His wisdom is complete and absolute. He needs no new experiences to expand it.

With us, however, there is a process involved. At birth the human mind is basically a blank slate. With time, knowledge, understanding, and wisdom begin to develop in the mind of a child.

For the sake of this book, let me give you my own simple definitions to these words that will explain this process. Please remember these are not theological definitions drawn from the original Hebrew text; they are just practical definitions that may help to understand the basics of this book.

Knowledge—knowing what the facts are
Understanding—knowing what the facts mean
Wisdom—knowing how the facts are applied

A child learns lots of things in the normal course of his or her existence. It takes time for a young mind to develop before the rapidly accumulating knowledge is joined by understanding. There is only so much that can be done to accelerate the process. Efforts can be made to teach a child, and those efforts can certainly help, but there is only so much a child is capable of at such a young age. It is admirable when parents and others attempt to stimulate young minds in creative ways so as to teach them to know and understand verbal and numerical concepts.

Wisdom is a bit more complex. It comes mostly with time and experience. It is no accident that in scripture, wisdom is associated with age. The young often have lots of knowledge but not so much wisdom. They can be very presumptuous, thinking that education has prepared them for everything. It takes time for knowledge and understanding to consolidate into wisdom.

The books of Proverbs and Ecclesiastes are the result of Solomon's life lived out with a supernatural infusion of godly wisdom, which resulted in a heightened awareness of all that was going on in and around Solomon's life. Others were incapable of processing observations the way Solomon did, because, through the lens of wisdom expressly given to him by God, he saw how life actually worked, and he wrote about his conclusions.

As we read the Bible, we should read it not only to establish our doctrines, give us comfort in times of trouble, or fulfill a requirement of Christian discipline; we also should read it as a guide that shows us how life is designed by God to work. We then learn to align our lives with the principles of God in such a way as to reap the continuous benefits of a life lived by divine design. Solomon tells us that the secret to true happiness is to find wisdom. It is better than financial riches when it comes to long-term fulfillment in life.

> *Happy is the man who finds wisdom, and the man who gains understanding; For her proceeds are better than the profits of silver, and her gain than fine gold.*
> Proverbs 3:13–14, NKJV

Knowledge

From the time we are born we begin to accumulate knowledge. We hear words, but at this point they are just sounds. Over time, those words begin to make sense when they are heard in the context of what they mean. Hearing the mother say such things as, *Mommy loves you, Mommy is coming, Mommy will take care of you,* gives context to the word *Mommy* as it is associated over and over again with the child's mother. Eventually, the child begins to formulate the word Mommy or Mama, doing so when the mother is around. The joyful smile the mother displays whenever she hears that word coming from the mouth of her child will encourage its use again and again.

Along with the learning of words comes the teaching of numbers. A parent teaches the child to memorize and recite mathematical equations such as $2+2=4$. The child may memorize that phrase before he/she even learns to count, and it will be a while before there is understanding of what the fact means. The child may be taught that 2+2=7. At this point, the child will not know the difference because he/she doesn't understand numbers at all. To the child, they are just words. Understanding will come later.

Understanding
Understanding emerges as the words and phrases the child has memorized become identified with the appropriate objects. They can then comprehend what the words mean. Simple numbers also begin to be understood. Over time it all begins to come together and make sense. Understanding is beginning to develop.

Wisdom
Wisdom eventually comes forth from knowledge and understanding as life's experiences present themselves in a way that requires knowledge and understanding to be applied in a beneficial way. Young people with lots of knowledge and a fair amount of understanding often assume these intellectual attainments equal wisdom. They argue with their elders using their oversimplified ideas and assumptions that to them seem very logical. As time goes by, they find (hopefully) through the process of trial and error that things are not as simple as they once thought. Time and experience produce further development of knowledge and understanding. Life tends to give more meaningful context to their knowledge. It's called wisdom.

IT'S ALL PART OF THE PROCESS

With God, I hasten to repeat, there is no process involved. He is the very essence of knowledge, understanding, and wisdom. It all comes from Him. As we have said, he is not learning. Experience is not making him wiser. He never has to rethink his assumptions. In fact, he has no assumptions. His wisdom is complete and absolute.

With people, it is a process. We must develop in these intellectual areas. Our development can be in a positive, beneficial direction of biblical wisdom, or it can go in the direction of the world's wisdom. That will ultimately determine what flows through our lives.

~ Chapter 6 ~

WISDOM, THE PRINCIPAL THING

*Wisdom is the principal thing; therefore get wisdom:
and with all thy getting get understanding.*
Proverbs 4:7

The book of Proverbs is, as we said earlier, truly inspired by God. It also is one of the most beloved books of the Bible.

As I briefly mentioned in chapter 2, my understanding of this amazing book has changed a bit over the years. Some of the promises that in my youth I thought were absolute, I now see as observations by the one who had a divine gift of observation. That, of course, is Solomon.

When a proverb says, "Train up a child in the way he should go, and when he is old, he will not depart from it" (Proverbs 22:6), I don't see it as a foundational, indisputable truth as much as a general observation. Too many people live in condemnation because their children turned out to be very different from how they were raised. The assumption can be that since your child did not turn out the way you hoped, you must have been a bad parent. The truth is there are factors in addition to parental guidance that form the character of children. There are more factors now than ever before—a lot more. With this in mind, parents must be very dedicated to the effort of raising their children in the way they should go, hoping to overcome all the negative influences that surround them.

The purpose of Proverbs is not to condemn parents who did their best to raise their children properly but found their efforts to come up short. What *is* the purpose of Proverbs then? If I were to put a subtitle on the book of Proverbs, it probably would be, *That's Just the Way It Works.* It is as though Solomon's message was, *I have watched, observed, studied, and experienced life from virtually every angle, and these are my conclusions. This, basically, is how it all works.*

THE PERSONIFICATION OF WISDOM

The main theme of the book of Proverbs is wisdom. Look at the words that introduce the book.

> *The proverbs of Solomon the son of David, king of Israel; To know wisdom and instruction; to perceive the words of understanding; To receive the instruction of wisdom, justice, and judgment, and equity.*
>
> *Proverbs 1:1–3*

As we have pointed out, Proverbs 1 personifies wisdom as a woman, and she voices the narrative. She basically says, *Here I am. Seek me, find me, appreciate me, learn from me. I have so much for you. You can benefit tremendously from what I can teach you.*

When I was young, I misunderstood the following portion of that first chapter:

> *I also will laugh at your calamity; I will mock when your fear cometh.*
>
> *Proverbs 1:26*

My misunderstanding had to do with who it is that laughs at our calamity. I used to think it was God. My view today is that God does not laugh at the bad things that happen to us; he grieves. So who is it that laughs at our calamities? Wisdom. Wisdom personified says, *I warned you. You could have known, you should have known, but you refused to pay attention, so I can't help but laugh.*

You know how that works. Suppose you warn someone about something, say, an icy spot just outside the door. He nonchalantly steps outside onto that slippery patch of ice. His feet fly in opposite directions, and down he goes. You look at him hoping he is not badly hurt, feeling obligated to show sympathy. But at the same time you're laughing yourself silly. You warned him; he should have taken heed and been more careful.

I don't think it was Solomon's intention to portray Wisdom as mean or vindictive, but as objective and impersonal. Wisdom can't believe her eyes when seeing us do what we should know better than to do. She shakes her head, chuckles, and says, *I tried to tell you, but you thought you knew better.*

THE TWO WOMEN OF PROVERBS

In the book of Proverbs there are two women who stand out to me.

The First Woman

She is Wisdom, the woman we've been talking about. Look at this passage.

> *Wisdom crieth without; she uttereth her voice in the streets: She crieth in the chief place of concourse, in the openings of the gates: in the city she uttereth her*

> words, saying, How long, ye simple ones, will ye love simplicity? and the scorners delight in their scorning, and fools hate knowledge?
>
> Proverbs 1:20–22

In these verses, we see this precious woman, Wisdom, speaking to us, admonishing us, warning us to listen carefully and take her words seriously. Her admonitions will save us from heartache if we will just listen, observe, and learn.

> Get wisdom, get understanding: forget it not; neither decline from the words of my mouth. Forsake her not, and she shall preserve thee: love her, and she shall keep thee. Wisdom is the principal thing; therefore get wisdom: and with all thy getting get understanding. Exalt her, and she shall promote thee: she shall bring thee to honour, when thou dost embrace her. She shall give to thine head an ornament of grace: a crown of glory shall she deliver to thee.
>
> Proverbs 4:5–9

In these verses this woman, Wisdom, is once again exalted and set forth as one to be listened to, one from which to learn. Her words are always the wisdom of God. They are the very foundation upon which the world is established. Because they are a faithful expression of the ways of God, they do not change. They are always true and can always be relied upon.

Her words are based upon the immutable word of God. She tells us to follow her teaching because we will be blessed if we do.

The Second Woman

In my view, this second woman typifies the wisdom of the world. She is introduced in Proverbs 2:16 and referred to in several subsequent verses (5:3, 20; 6:24; 7:5) as the "strange woman."

> *For the lips of a strange woman drop as an honeycomb, and her mouth is smoother than oil: But her end is bitter as wormwood, sharp as a twoedged sword. Her feet go down to death; her steps take hold on hell. Lest thou shouldest ponder the path of life, her ways are moveable, that thou canst not know them. Hear me now therefore, O ye children, and depart not from the words of my mouth. Remove thy way far from her, and come not nigh the door of her house.*
>
> Proverbs 5:3–8

A Brief Note of Clarification

Because the natural world and the spiritual world mirror each other in many ways, Bible verses can so often have double meanings: one having to do with our natural, earthly lives and one relating to our spiritual lives. This "strange woman" in Proverbs is one example. We are warned in these verses of the dangers of being lured into immoral relationships, a scenario of the earthly dimension that can happen to men and women alike. I believe that this "strange woman" can also be seen as the opposite of the woman called Wisdom. The two women are thus a portrayal of the wisdom of God as opposed to the wisdom of the world.

Back to the Subject at Hand
The King James Version uses the word *strange* in describing this woman. Other versions use words like *immoral, seductive, forbidden, adulterous,* and possibly others. Each of these words would easily fit into the explanation set forth in the following paragraphs.

The wisdom of the world is the antithesis of the wisdom of God. The woman who is called Wisdom in Proverbs is the opposite of the "strange woman" in the same book. Whereas the wisdom of God leads to blessing, the wisdom of the world leads to bitterness, defeat, and death.

Let me insert a New Testament verse into this discussion.

> *Beware lest any man spoil you through philosophy and vain deceit, after the tradition of men, after the rudiments of the world, and not after Christ.*
> *Colossians 2:8*

A brief look at this verse in Colossians shows us that the wisdom or philosophy of the world will spoil us. What does *spoil* mean? Once again, we see a King James Version word that is not ordinarily used in this context today. Other versions set forth words like *cheat, capture,* or *rob*. The message here is that the world's wisdom and philosophies will rob you of what you have in terms of your faith.

Let's look at these verses in Proverbs 5 and Colossians 2 to see how they relate.

The words of the "strange woman" in Proverbs are sweet, smooth, and seductive. She lures her prey into her lair, promising one thing and delivering another. She promises love, pleasure, and fulfilment, but delivers death and destruction.

Paul, in Colossians 2, refers to "vain deceit." In a moment, I will expand on this, but for now, let me continue looking at these two women of Proverbs.

As Wisdom speaks, her words are immortalized in the word of God, "forever settled" as the psalmist puts it (See Psalm 119:89). Her words are always relevant, always true. They span the generations, giving advice and counsel that is always applicable to people's lives.

The strange woman's ways, on the other hand, are moveable (as stated in the verses above). They cannot be known. Why? Because they constantly change.

Consider the term "conventional wisdom." This is the wisdom of the day. It is probably different from what was stated yesterday and most likely will change again tomorrow. The world's wisdom or philosophy is moveable, constantly changing. To be current with the prevailing declarations of what is right, wrong, and true in the eyes of the world requires an almost daily attention to the purveyors of acceptable thought. What is declared to be right and acceptable today may be reversed tomorrow. You just never know.

WHAT IS VAIN DECEIT AND HOW DOES IT WORK?

Other commentators may disagree with the following explanations and conclusions regarding *vain deceit*. That doesn't mean they are wrong and I am right any more than it means they are right and I am wrong. This is simply my understanding. You be the judge.

In my view, *vain deceit* is deceit or deception that appeals to one's vanity.

I realize that other translations use the word *empty* rather than *vain*. There is a certain emptiness in personal vanity. People who are considered vain are often thought of as empty, shallow, vacuous.

The verse containing the words *vain deceit* reminds me of the encounter between Eve and the serpent in the Garden of Eden.

> *For God doth know that in the day ye eat thereof, then your eyes shall be opened, and ye shall be as gods, knowing good and evil.*
>
> Genesis 3:5

The serpent had observed Eve looking at the tree containing the forbidden fruit and began to question her regarding God's instruction and warning to her and her husband, Adam. Ultimately, the serpent appealed to her vanity. Here is my paraphrase of what the serpent said to Eve as found in Genesis 3:1-5.

> *What is it, Eve, that convinces you that someone else should make decisions about what is right and wrong for you? You must realize that God is simply attempting to keep you under his thumb. I'm telling you that if you eat of this fruit, you will not die. In fact, you will become like God. You will then be able to determine for yourself what is right and wrong. No one can know that better than you. Not even God.*

Does this sound familiar? Of course, it does. We hear it every day. People are drawn into the same kind of deception as Eve was.

The serpent appealed to the vanity of Eve. *You are just as smart as God*, Satan implied. *All you have to do is accept what I say rather than what God says. What I say will set you free, free to be you!*

So today we have people constantly arguing against what God has declared in his word, substituting their own declarations and their own wisdom for His.

THEREFORE, GET WISDOM

So, the admonition of the book of Proverbs is to get wisdom. Not the wisdom of the world, of course, but the wisdom from God and his word. Get the wisdom that is based upon the very principles of creation law. That wisdom is the real key to a happy, prosperous life.

Why? Because *that's just the way it works*.

~ Chapter 7 ~

THE FLOW OF CREATION

Have you ever wondered how God's creation seems to continue from year to year, decade to decade, century to century? What has kept all of it going for thousands of years? Wars, disease, famines, and natural disasters—earthquakes, volcanoes, floods, droughts, hurricanes, tornadoes—and any number of other crises have occurred regularly over the centuries, yet the earth continues to rotate on its axis and revolve around the sun as if none of it has happened. Mankind has never been wiped out. Grass, trees, and other vegetation continue to flourish. Animal life survives all those events as well.

A VERY MEMORABLE PERSONAL EXPERIENCE

On June 9, 1972, my wife Julie, our infant daughter Christy, and I were in Rapid City, South Dakota, visiting some friends and relatives. We had lived there for a year and a half just after my graduation from Bible college, helping to launch a new church. It had been about six months since we had left to travel in evangelistic ministry, and we just happened to pass back through on our way to California.

It was a very cloudy day with rain falling intermittently throughout the afternoon and evening. Nothing unusual. None of us had any idea that up in the Black Hills just west of the city torrential rains were falling, filling lakes and streams. Ultimately, all of this water flowed into Canyon Lake, a manmade lake on the west side of Rapid City. Late that evening the dam that held the water in the lake collapsed, emptying the lake into and through Rapid City.

It was a horrible night—buildings washed away, large portions of asphalt parking lots stacked up like pieces of paper, cars carried away, railroad tracks dislodged and twisted like drinking straws. Worst of all, 238 people lost their lives. It all took probably less than an hour.

Early the next morning several of us went out to survey the damage and search for survivors. Unfortunately, what we found were people who had died in their cars, in their houses, and even in trees. We helped retrieve bodies from cars so they could be taken to funeral homes where they would be laid out in rows to await identification.

The word *surreal* is often used to describe such experiences. One day everything is fine, just going along normally, and then without warning catastrophe strikes, wiping out hundreds of lives. The following day the rain has stopped, the sun is out, the clouds are gone, and in nature all things continue as if nothing happened.

This isolated personal experience is just one of thousands that show us how uncertain life can be. We have no guarantees that our lives will be free from disaster or other life-threatening events. And yet, as we look at the big picture and despite all these terrible things, life seems to go on.

Losing 238 people in one hour's time as happened that night in Rapid City is horrible, yet other natural disasters in other places have wiped out thousands upon thousands in earthquakes, tsunamis, tornadoes, and hurricanes.

It happens. As far as I know, there is no philosophical answer as to why. People speculate, setting forth all kinds of interesting explanations: it's the judgment of God; it's climate change; it's solar flares; it's the current moon phase. Who knows? I'm sure I don't.

One thing I do know is that there are no promises in the Bible of a life without problems. Even aligning ourselves perfectly with God's creation laws will not insulate us from problems. What it will do, though, is guarantee us a flow of blessing that will ultimately get us through whatever life casts our way, whether good or bad.

ALL OF GOD'S CREATION FLOWS

There is movement in everything. Nothing is ever static or completely motionless. Nothing.

Ecclesiastes 1 gives an interesting description of how everything has a distinct flow. Let's read a few verses.

> *One generation passeth away, and another generation cometh: but the earth abideth for ever. The sun also ariseth, and the sun goeth down, and hasteth to his place where he arose. The wind goeth toward the south, and turneth about unto the north; it whirleth about continually, and the wind returneth again according to his circuits. All the rivers run into the sea; yet the sea is not full; unto the place from whence the rivers come, thither they return again. All things are full of labour; man cannot utter it: the eye is not satisfied with seeing, nor the ear filled with hearing. The thing that hath been, it is that which shall be; and that which is done is that which shall be done: and there is no new*

thing under the sun. Is there any thing whereof it may be said, See, this is new? it hath been already of old time, which was before us. There is no remembrance of former things; neither shall there be any remembrance of things that are to come with those that shall come after.

Ecclesiastes 1:4–11

These verses in Ecclesiastes show a distinctive movement, a flow of God's creation. Let's look at these references.

Generational Flow. One generation flows into another such that one can scarcely tell when one generation ends and another begins. The generations move along in a continual flow. One is always starting; one is always ending. Humanity just keeps on going.

Sunrise, Sunset. It's as dependable as anything can be. Throughout all of earth's history the sun has arisen in the east and set in the west. Regardless of where you may be on Planet Earth, it is totally predictable. You can count on it happening every day. One day flows into another, as a new day starts every hour somewhere on the planet.

Air Currents. Wind is air moving continuously around the earth. It never stops. At times the wind blows with gale force while at other times it is a gentle breeze. Sometimes it may seem as though there is no movement at all but make no mistake; the flow of air never stops.

Water Movement. What about the rivers? Why are the oceans and seas never full even though large rivers are forever emptying themselves there? Why don't the rivers run dry? It is because of the flow established in the atmosphere called the water cycle in which water is continually evaporating and being carried by wind currents to every part of the globe. Water evaporated out of the Gulf of Mexico eventually finds its way north where rain and snow fall. It then flows back into the rivers and makes the same southward journey to the Gulf of Mexico. The cycle never stops. The same law governs both the northern and the southern hemispheres.

Nothing Is Ever Really New. Why did the wise writer say there is nothing new under the sun? Because there is a flow that is established in our world that continually recycles everything. All the "new ideas" you hear of arise from something that has already been known. New inventions are usually just improvements or variations of something that has already been invented.

> *For precept must be upon precept, precept upon precept; line upon line, line upon line; here a little, and there a little.*
>
> Isaiah 28:10

THE FLOW OF GOD'S WORD

Let me carry this a little further. The Bible is divided into two distinct parts: the Old Testament and the New Testament. No one argues about that. It is interesting that some people seem to think these two parts are totally separate. One part is mostly irrelevant since the other came along and replaced it. The New Testament is for us today, and the Old Testament is obsolete.

I would like to point out, though, that just as one generation flows into another and one day flows into another, the Old Testament flowed into the New Testament. Just as every generation contains vestiges of every previous generation, the New Testament contains vestiges of the Old Testament. Just as new generations could never exist without generations past, the New Testament could not exist without the Old. The Old Testament was not done away with; it was the very basis or foundation for everything that is in the New Testament. While we may not live our lives strictly *by* the Old Testament, we need to know that a thorough understanding of the New truly depends upon a good knowledge of the Old.

In the New Testament, when Jesus referred to *the scriptures*, he was referencing something in the Old Testament. When Paul referred to *the scriptures*, he also was citing something in the Old Testament.

One of the reasons that the Jews were so instrumental in formulating New Testament doctrine was their understanding of Old Testament writings. This is because the New Testament is not a body of writings completely divorced from the Old Testament, but a designed outflow of it.

The Old Testament was fulfilled in Jesus Christ. The principles of Old Testament law were the basis for Jesus' ministry on the earth. The elements of the law—the priesthood, the sacrifices, the altar, the blood, as well as a host of other things—culminated in the life, ministry, death, burial, and resurrection of Jesus. From that point forward all the principles of the law continued but did not have to be ceremonially repeated by us because Jesus was the one in whom all things were fulfilled. His fulfillment of those law requirements was once and for all. From that point, we only had to look to Jesus to have our sins forgiven. He paid the price for us all. Thus, New Testament life is the result of Old Testament fulfillment. The two cannot be completely separated; one testament flows into the other, giving us "The Bible."

THE IMPORTANCE OF UNDERSTANDING THE FLOW

In this book, *That's Just the Way It Works*, one of the important features I'm attempting to explain is this idea of a continual, unstoppable flow of virtually everything in creation.

In subsequent chapters, we will show scripturally how we generate the flow of blessings into our lives for the benefit of ourselves and those around us.

~ Chapter 8 ~
UNDERSTANDING THE FLOW OF SPIRITUAL THINGS

CREATION IN MOTION

In chapter 7, "The Flow of Creation," we used Ecclesiastes 1:4–11 to present a brief description of the flow of physical life on earth. It is my belief that the laws of the physical world and the laws of the spiritual world are very much the same. Based upon this similarity, Jesus used natural, physical examples to explain spiritual truths.

In his teachings we see Jesus saying such things as, *The kingdom of heaven is like* . . . and then equating the kingdom of heaven to things in the natural world. Things such as a grain of mustard seed, leaven, a treasure hidden in a field, a merchant man seeking quality pearls, a net cast into the sea, an owner of a vineyard, a king hosting a wedding for his son—all are examples of things we know about in the natural world, but they are to be understood as explanations of spiritual-world truths.

In still other places we find agriculture (sowing and reaping), livestock (sheep), family, building (architecture), the human body (the body of Christ), fishing (fishers of men), citizenry (fellow citizens), and money (talents), all used to describe some aspect of the kingdom or the church.

All of this serves as a basis for understanding what we are calling "the flow" as it pertains to the natural world *and* the spiritual world. In other words, just as there is a continual flow in the natural world, there also is a flow in the spiritual world.

Here are some explanations from scripture.

THE MOTIONS OF SINS

As I was reading in Romans 7, a phrase grabbed my attention. It was *the motions of sins*.

> *For when we were in the flesh, the motions of sins, which were by the law, did work in our members to bring forth fruit unto death.*
>
> *Romans 7:5*

Admittedly, the King James Version is one of the few places where I found this phrase, *the motions of sins*. Although other versions do not use the word *motions*, several use words such as *sinful passions*, *sinful cravings*, and *the stirrings of sin*. Once again, I remind you that I am not interested in developing some novel theology or using a particular biblical phrase out of context to set forth some strange theory.

I mention this verse because it struck me that sin is an active force that does not affect just one person. It can affect many others besides the one who actually commits the sin. In fact, it virtually always does.

Passions, cravings, and stirrings are all words that suggest activity. Sin is active. It tends to beget more sin. It's like cancer; it grows and spreads.

I include this negative aspect of motion and flow only to reinforce the understanding that everything in creation is in motion all the time. Whether it is the flow of sin and its destructive forces, or the flow of spiritual blessings in our lives, everything is in motion.

With all this in mind, I direct your thinking to another kind of flow, the kind we generate in our lives by the way we live.

THE FLOW GENERATED BY GIVING

Much of what comes our way in life has to do with the choices we make. We initiate the flow of good things or bad things by what we do, the things we say, the paths we take, and the attitudes we develop and display. For an explanation, we'll start in the book of Luke.

> *Give, and it shall be given unto you; good measure, pressed down, and shaken together, and running over, shall men give into your bosom. For with the same measure that ye mete withal it shall be measured to you again.*
>
> *Luke 6:38*

This verse is often quoted when people are being asked to give money to some ministry, building project, or other church-related need. While it is true that money can fit into this explanation, it is only a small part of the promise. The monetary aspect will be looked at later, but let's take a few moments to look at the full scope of what the promise of this verse entails.

We will not list all the relevant verses that precede Luke 6:38, but here is a list of several things that are mentioned there. Going back as far as verse 27 we find words and phrases such as *love, do good, bless, pray for, lend, turn the other cheek, give, be merciful, and forgive.* These are all positive virtues and actions that everyone can engage in. Also mentioned, however, are *cursing, judgment, and condemnation.*

So the question might be this: When the Bible says, "Give and it shall be given," what does *it* refer to? The answer is simple; *it* refers to whatever you give. Whatever you give shall be given to you. When you give of yourself to others—love, blessing, mercy, forgiveness, and such—you generate a flow of those very things back into your own life.

The same is true of cursing, judgment, and condemnation. People who curse (as opposed to bless), judge, and condemn are often met with the same attitudes they display.

We tend to get what we give.

A person who is loving tends to be loved. A merciful, forgiving, tolerant, kind, considerate person tends to be the recipient of those same virtues.

How do people usually respond to happy, positive, smiling people? Most of the time, people find themselves returning those very feelings and expressions back to the person. Happy, smiling people tend to light up a room, and people in that room are drawn to them.

This is a very simple explanation of how we create a flow of blessing in our lives.

THE FLOW OF THE HOLY SPIRIT

> *He that believeth on me, as the scripture hath said, out of his belly shall flow rivers of living water. (But this*

> spake he of the Spirit, which they that believe on him should receive: for the Holy Ghost was not yet given; because that Jesus was not yet glorified.)
>
> John 7:38–39

> And when he had said this, he breathed on them, and saith unto them, Receive ye the Holy Ghost.
>
> John 20:22

> And they were all filled with the Holy Ghost, and began to speak with other tongues, as the Spirit gave them utterance.
>
> Acts 2:4

For most of my life I thought of the importance of *receiving* the Holy Ghost, or as others prefer, the Holy Spirit. In John 20:22, Jesus instructed the disciples to receive the Holy Ghost. In Acts 2:4, we see where they actually did receive it.

I noticed, however, that when Jesus spoke of the Holy Ghost in John 7:38, he stated, "Out of his belly [innermost being], would flow rivers of living water." It was after I had begun to contemplate this idea of the flow we generate in our own lives that this verse popped out at me.

The Holy Spirit is not intended to flow into us to be housed, stored, or bottled up, but to flow out of us, touching and blessing those around us. The more it flows out of us, the more it flows into us. It is that continuous flow that keeps God's Spirit fresh and alive in us. The more we give to others of the gift within us, the more we will have to give.

NOW, ABOUT THAT MONEY THING

One of the more controversial aspects of the *give and it shall be given* concept presents itself when someone uses it in reference to financial giving—you know, money. This principle should not be used to entice people to give by promising that their gift will generate some kind of miraculous windfall of cash from unknown sources in a few days.

It is important to understand that we generate a flow of blessing by the good things we give. It's true even when money is being given, especially when given in love and support of worthy and godly causes. While time and space do not allow a complete list of verses that support this view, let's look at just a few. Some are Old Testament verses while others are from the New Testament.

The first verse is the main one that is used to encourage people to give tithes and offerings. The promises are significant and specific.

> *Bring ye all the tithes into the storehouse, that there may be meat in mine house, and prove me now herewith, saith the LORD of hosts, if I will not open you the windows of heaven, and pour you out a blessing, that there shall not be room enough to receive it. And I will rebuke the devourer for your sakes, and he shall not destroy the fruits of your ground; neither shall your vine cast her fruit before the time in the field, saith the LORD of hosts.*
>
> Malachi 3:10–11

The verses preceding the ones cited above state that the people who were withholding tithes and offerings were actually robbing God. As a result, they were living under a curse. What was the curse? The closing of the windows of heaven. It could be said that the people stopped the flow of blessings that would have been generated by their faithfulness in tithes and offerings. But God promised that if they resumed their giving, the result would be that he would reopen the windows of heaven and pour out a blessing greater than they could receive. This brings to mind Luke's words *good measure, pressed down, shaken together*. The message was that it was up to them to do what was necessary to generate the flow of blessings from heaven.

Just a couple more verses, this time from the New Testament.

> *I have shewed you all things, how that so labouring ye ought to support the weak, and to remember the words of the Lord Jesus, how he said,* **It is more blessed to give than to receive.**
>
> Acts 20:35 (emphasis added)

> *But this I say, He which soweth sparingly shall reap also sparingly; and he which soweth bountifully shall reap also bountifully. Every man according as he purposeth in his heart, so let him give; not grudgingly, or of necessity:* **for God loveth a cheerful giver.**
>
> 2 Corinthians 9:6–7 (emphasis added)

Please note the highlighted portions of these verses. The first one is the well-known statement, *It is more blessed to give than to receive.* It could be said that more blessing is generated by giving than by receiving. The giving principle is not just to make the giver feel all warm and happy inside, though that certainly can be the case. It means the act of giving generates a flow of blessing back to the giver. You know, *Give and it shall be given*. Receiving is wonderful, but it is the giving that generates the flow of blessing.

The next verse also contains a well-known, stand-alone adage: *For God loveth a cheerful giver*. I believe that when a person loves to give, and gives cheerfully, God seems to (in some ways hard to understand) make certain that the giver has the means to continue giving.

CASH FLOW

Cash flow is an economic term that pertains to the natural world of commerce, but also to the spiritual world of giving. If everyone quit spending money, the world's economy would eventually grind to a halt. Spending keeps cash flowing, and as a result, increases the amount of cash in the system. The flow of cash in the economy generates more cash. It's a fact.

In the New Testament parable of the talents (Matthew 25:14–28), Jesus spoke of three servants, each of whom was entrusted with a certain number of talents (a monetary term). The master left instructions with the servants to invest the money—get it into the marketplace so it would increase in value. Two of the three did so, but the third hid his talent for fear he would lose it. The two investors saw a return on their investments, which they presented back to the master. Both of these servants were commended for their faithfulness. The one who refused to put his portion out into the marketplace was condemned. He still had the original amount that had been given to him, but because he buried it, it generated no return. So what he had been given was taken away.

I've observed that people get very concerned when they think you're attempting to get into their pocketbook. I understand that. No one wants to be taken advantage of regarding their money, including me. Believing you will receive a commensurate return by giving away various virtues like love, mercy, and others is one thing; but the notion that when you give tithes and offerings you might ultimately end up with more money than you had originally is a stretch.

So, at the risk of seeming to press the issue too far, here are a couple of additional verses that speak to the issue.

> *Honour the LORD with thy substance, and with the firstfruits of all thine increase: So shall thy barns be filled with plenty, and thy presses shall burst out with new wine.*
>
> Proverbs 3:9–10

> *There is that scattereth, and yet increaseth; and there is that withholdeth more than is meet, but it tendeth to poverty.*
>
> Proverbs 11:24

A Brief Pause for a Personal Testimony

Several years ago Julie and I attempted to start a church in a small South Dakota town. We were very young, quite inexperienced, and virtually alone. Looking back, we wonder how we survived. When we arrived in town, all we had was a few items that we loaded into the smallest U-Haul trailer available. During that time

I took whatever jobs I could find while Julie stayed home with our daughter, Christy, and later, our son, Michael, who was born while we were there. In addition to attempting to support ourselves, we also contributed to the support of our fledgling church. We received no money from the church, but we faithfully gave our tithes and offerings into the church. After five years, we assumed a pastorate in another South Dakota city, leaving a small group of people who had started coming to our church. As we were packing a large truck with our furniture, Julie and I looked at each other in amazement. How did we accumulate all this nice furniture?! Our answer was simple: it was the blessing of the Lord.

Our story is not that unusual. In fact, I would venture to say that several people who are reading these words could tell similar stories. Why? Because the blessings of the Lord flow into the lives of faithful people.

IT'S NOT THE MONEY, IT'S THE PRINCIPLE

You've heard it said, "When someone says, 'It's not the money, it's the principle,' you know it's the money." Right? Not always, because in the context of this discussion it really is the principle. My desire is not to get into someone's bank account or to entice someone to give me or anyone else money if they choose not to give. It is simply to demonstrate how I have come to view life and how it works. The principle of giving and receiving is part of that package.

Is my existence merely a bunch of random, mindless choices made in the hope that somehow everything will work out? Or is there rhyme and reason to this world? Can I follow some basic rules of life that will produce good results that will make my life happier and more successful?

It is my view that God has created the world to work the way it does, and if I learn those ways and principles, I can align myself with that divine design in such a way as to benefit from God's great plan.

Maybe some of the words of this book will resonate with others as well.

A WORD OF CLARIFICATION

In specific instances, one may show love and be hurt in return. Or one may forgive but not be forgiven by an offended party. Likewise, a person may be faithful in tithes and offerings but nonetheless experience financial difficulties.

None of the above declarations can be guaranteed in every instance. There are many variables. We are not robots, and the people around us are not preprogrammed to act according to God's design. We must always recognize that many people around us live by a value system not taught in scripture. Over a period of time, however, when people practice love, mercy, forgiveness, and other such virtues, a flow of these same virtues generally is produced in their lives.

Remember the words of Jesus in Matthew 10:8: "Freely ye have received, freely give."

It's all a part of God's design.

~ Chapter 9 ~

JUDGMENT VS. CONSEQUENCES

You may remember the old country song (Written by E.E. Collins, sung by George Jones and Tammy Wynette) that so completely described some people's belief about God's judgment and how it is meted out. The lyrics said, *God's gonna getcha for that.* In other words, God is just waiting for us to make a mistake at which time he will get us and get us good.

On the other hand, in today's church environment you hear a lot about legalism. The subject usually arises when one thinks some things should be required of Christians and others don't agree. Sometimes the claim of legalism is valid; at other times it can simply be a blanket approval or rejection of whatever one wants to do or not do.

In simple theological terms, *legalism* is salvation by works. It is based upon the idea that some people and some churches require various things for salvation that the Bible does not require. There are many variations of this view.

While few people consider themselves legalists, there are those who tend to consider nearly everyone legalists but themselves.

At this point the argument about grace arises in theological discussions regarding what people should and should not do or what they must believe to be saved.

This is probably a good place to draw a distinction between the *God will never let you get away with that* and the *grace covers it all* doctrines. My purpose in this book is not to deal with either extreme but to draw a distinction between the judgment of God and the natural consequences that result from the things we do.

One of the most quoted verses in the Bible regarding salvation by grace is found in the book of Ephesians.

> *For by grace are ye saved through faith; and that not of yourselves: it is the gift of God: Not of works, lest any man should boast.*
>
> Ephesians 2:8–9

While no serious Christian would argue the truth of that verse, some may interpret it differently. What are "works"? To many, almost anything that could or would be required of anyone in the context of Christianity would be considered *works*, especially as it relates to salvation.

Personally, I don't want to argue about whether things like baptism (one of the subjects that often arises), as well as others, should be considered as works in this book, even though I consider baptism to be of utmost importance. A discussion of this is for another time. I do know, however, that whatever the "works of righteousness" may be, we are not saved by them.

> *But after that the kindness and love of God our Saviour toward man appeared, Not by works of righteousness which we have done, but according to his mercy he saved us, by the washing of regeneration, and renewing of the Holy Ghost; Which he shed on us abundantly through Jesus Christ our Saviour; That being justified by his grace, we should*

> *be made heirs according to the hope of eternal life.*
> *Titus 3:4–7*

In other words, we are saved not just by being good people or doing good deeds. We are saved by our faith in Jesus Christ and our acceptance of what he did for us that we could never have done for ourselves. Yes, salvation is a gift; it's free. We cannot buy it with money or anything else that we might consider an acceptable exchange. Jesus paid it all on the cross. Most Christians believe that. I know I do.

That being said, once we are saved, should we do certain things in order to please God? Of course. God wants us to live life as he designed it, and he is pleased when we do. Good things happen when we live life that way.

CONSIDERING THE ISSUE OF PLEASING GOD

The idea of legalism is legitimate, and we must not add requirements for salvation that are not found in scripture. We are, however, instructed to do certain things after we are saved that cannot be labeled as legalistic—things that please the Lord. Consider the following verses that have to do with pleasing God and how we can do so.

> *For it is God which worketh in you both to will and to do of his good pleasure.*
> *Philippians 2:13*

> *Now the God of peace, that brought again from the dead our Lord Jesus, that great shepherd of the sheep,*

> *through the blood of the everlasting covenant, make you perfect in every good work to do his will, working in you that which is well-pleasing in his sight, through Jesus Christ; to whom be glory for ever and ever. Amen.*
> Hebrews 13:20–21

Please note the words in these two references: *it is God which worketh in you*, and *the great shepherd . . . working in you*. I love knowing that our efforts to please God are facilitated by God himself. He works in us and through us, enabling us to do the things that are well pleasing to him.

Some things please God; other things grieve him. We should seek to know what things grieve the Spirit of God as well as those that please him.

> *And grieve not the holy Spirit of God, whereby ye are sealed unto the day of redemption.*
> Ephesians 4:30

These verses have nothing to do with legalism and everything to do with the individual's relationship with God and how it can be enhanced or damaged. So, even though in this chapter we are exploring the difference between the judgment of God and natural consequences, there also is a concern for things that please or displease God.

RED FLAGS EVERYWHERE

I can see them from here, believe me. Many people have the view that once they are saved, they must follow a long list of rules and regulations designed to keep them saved. If they don't follow them religiously, God will wreak judgment upon them. Thus, following those rules, in some people's minds, enables them to stay saved.

Growing up, I remember thinking my salvation hung by a thread. One wrong move and I could lose my soul forever. If the *rapture* were to take place, I would miss it. While this fear probably kept me from doing some bad things, the motivation behind my good behavior was flawed. I certainly don't wish I had done those "bad" things, but I do wish I had understood my position in Jesus Christ a bit better.

IS GRACE A FREE RIDE?

A few doctrinal positions exist that are more fanciful than scriptural. Take the concept of grace, for example. The standard definition of the word is *the unmerited favor of God*. There is nothing wrong with that. In fact, I believe it and teach it. I refuse, however, to build my entire view of this subject upon five words. Grace must be understood not just by a dictionary definition, but in scriptural context. Take the book of Ephesians, for example, the same book that tells us we are saved by grace.

The book of Ephesians can be divided into two distinct parts. The first part (chapters 1–3) focuses on our position in Christ and the blessings derived from that position. These chapters declare many things about who Jesus is, what the church is, and what is available to us in Christ, as well as other wonderful spiritual realities.

The second part (chapters 4–6) contains virtually nothing but instructions about things we should and should not do.

So what happened here? Did Paul spend the first three chapters of the book of Ephesians extolling the virtues of grace only to suddenly turn into a legalist in chapters 4–6, spouting a list of dos and don'ts? I don't think so, and I doubt that you think so either.

Whether or not one is a Christian, life still works the way it works. Natural laws of life are in effect regardless of one's relationship to God.

The Christian is still subject to the law of gravity.

The Christian still must eat, drink, sleep, and breathe to stay alive.

If the Christian touches a hot stove, his or her hand will burn.

The Christian can still get chicken pox, measles, cancer, and have heart attacks.

A Christian's relationship issues regarding family and friends still tend to be the same.

I could go on, but you understand what I'm saying.

The point is that when Paul filled the last three chapters of Ephesians with instructions, it was to provide us an understanding of several things: how we should walk, how we should talk, and how we should conduct ourselves in the various interpersonal relationships that are common to us all. I do not see these instructions as rules and regulations; they are instructions in wisdom. They help us to live our lives positively and productively. And that is pleasing to God.

IS IT A SIN?

Is it a sin to drink alcohol? Is it a sin to smoke? Is it a sin to dance? Is it a sin to dress certain ways? What about "mixed bathing?" (For those in the younger generation, that was the term used by many denominations for men, women, boys, and girls all swimming together. Yeah, I know . . . go ahead and laugh. I'm actually laughing myself.)

Years ago, several of these things as well as many others were commonly a part of the list of mandatory standards and rules of many mainline denominations included in their articles of faith. Teaching these things as sin led people to believe that one could not be saved if he or she engaged in these "sinful" activities. Over time, people began to push back against these prohibitions, saying that because we are saved by grace, anything that would be added as requirements for salvation such as these rules was nothing but legalism, and therefore to be discarded. Over time, most of these rules or standards were abandoned. As a result, the pendulum has swung from the point where some saw that nearly everything was wrong to the opposite point where some consider that almost nothing is wrong.

So what about those things? Is there a reason to avoid certain activities?

My answer is yes, not because of the judgment of God that might fall upon us as punishment, but because of the natural consequences of certain things we might do.

We should all know the dangers of smoking, drinking, drug use, sexual promiscuity, lying, cheating, stealing, and many other things that are illegal, dangerous, or at the least ill-advised. God, however, is not on patrol looking for violations of his religious standards so he can arrest us, condemn us, and punish us for breaking his law. He has simply created a world that incorporates certain laws based upon his incalculable wisdom. We do certain things, and automatic consequences ensue. *That's just the way it works.*

If I were to caution people in my teaching about certain things, it would not be to exert control over their lives or to infringe upon their freedom; it would be to protect them from some of the inevitable results of ill-advised choices.

This is not about judgment; it is about consequences. The things we do incur inevitable results. That is not to say there is no divine judgment. The Bible refers to the judgment of God in many places, so don't misunderstand me here. It is just that many of our choices do not require individual responses from God, such as blessings and rewards for doing good and punishment for doing bad.

I, as well as many others, have cited a verse in the book of Numbers many times over the years.

> *Behold, ye have sinned against the L*ORD*: and be sure your sin will find you out.*
>
> Numbers 32:23

I must confess that many years ago I placed that verse in the context of *God's gonna getcha for that*. Or, *You'll never get away with it; God will see to that*. One day, however, it occurred to me that the verse specifically said, *Your sin will find you out*, not that *God will find you out*. That insight brought me to the conclusion that sin can and does carry with it its own consequences, and not necessarily the specific, targeted judgment of God. This is one more indication that God has created the world to work the way it does. The more we understand what that ultimate plan of wisdom is, the more able we are to generate the flow of blessing in our lives by making good choices as taught in God's word.

ARE THERE JUDGMENTS AND REWARDS?

Good question. The answer? Absolutely. But we'll get to that in a moment.

It is not my intention to make it seem as if God has designed life to be some kind of a cookie-cutter existence where everyone does all the same things. We can make a million choices and still be within the parameters of God's wisdom.

Please don't take away from this book the idea that a blessed life is the automatic result of just *getting it all right*. The grace and mercy of Jesus Christ is there for all of us. No one does everything perfectly. Everyone battles against the tendency to yield to fleshly desires. That is why we need a close personal relationship with the Lord. His forgiveness, his protection, his guidance, and his understanding of us as humans are all important to us in our journey on this earth.

> *All we like sheep have gone astray; we have turned every one to his own way; and the LORD hath laid on him the iniquity of us all.*
>
> Isaiah 53:6

Can I say it one more time? *No one gets it all right!* No one makes all the right choices. No one is perfect. Like sheep, we all have the tendency to wander, often straying from the pasture God has provided. It's human nature, and we are all human.

The beauty of the Christian life is that even when we do stray, we have the assurance that the judgment and penalty for our transgressions have been laid upon Jesus Christ. Just as we received forgiveness for our sins when we first came to the Lord, we continue to receive forgiveness for the sins we commit afterward.

See what the apostle John tells us in his first epistle.

> *If we say that we have no sin, we deceive ourselves, and the truth is not in us. If we confess our sins, He is faithful and just to forgive us our sins and to cleanse us from all unrighteousness. If we say that we have not sinned, we make Him a liar, and His word is not in us.*
> 1 John 1:8–10, NKJV

We have wonderful promises that guarantee us that even though we sin we have forgiveness from the one who paid the ultimate price for our redemption. Jesus has provided a complete plan not only for our salvation, but for our continued growth toward maturity and perfection in him.

REWARDS? YES

> *But love ye your enemies, and do good, and lend, hoping for nothing again; and your reward shall be great, and ye shall be the children of the Highest: for he is kind unto the unthankful and to the evil.*
> Luke 6:35

Certainly, there are rewards for doing the right thing, just as parents reward their children with extra allowance when they get good grades on their report card or complete their chores in a timely fashion. Schools honor students who have perfect attendance or those who stay out of trouble.

Some of those rewards for our actions will be given in heaven ("great is your reward in heaven"—Matthew 5:12); others will be obtained as mere results of doing the right things.

Let me reiterate that this is not a theology book. It is not a book of dos and don'ts. It is not a book of absolutes. It is not a "do it my way or else" book. It is not a "this is how you stay saved" book. It is not a book that promotes a certain doctrine. It is a book designed to gently explain why things in life work the way they do.

Whatever denomination you belong to, whatever religion you are, even if you are an atheist, human nature is human nature. And believe me, human nature and the inherent laws of creation override any sectarian belief that one has accepted. The laws of human nature have never changed, and they never will be changed.

WHAT ABOUT JUDGMENT?

We all know the judgment of God is a reality. Anyone who reads the Bible knows about "the judgment seat of Christ" (2 Corinthians 5:10) and the judgment at the "great white throne" (Revelation 20:11), both of which are end-time judgments. They are real.

The subject of this book, however, does not include these types of judgments that are ultimately meted out by God. The main objective of this book is to help all of us understand how life works as designed by God. It's about things such as sowing and reaping, building our houses/lives upon the solid rock, and ordering our lives according to God's wisdom. It is about an understanding of the natural laws God has incorporated into creation, why they are there, and how they work.

Again, it's not about a legalistic life led for the purpose of being saved; it's about living our lives in ways that produce a flow of blessing into us that extends to those around us, which ultimately pleases God.

The judgment of God is, in my view, different from this. And although it is a vital subject to be dealt with, I choose not to do so here.

~ Chapter 10 ~

SPIRIT, SOUL, AND BODY

*And the very God of peace sanctify you wholly; and I pray
God your whole spirit and soul and body be preserved
blameless unto the coming of our Lord Jesus Christ.*
1 Thessalonians 5:23

I remember hearing Paul Harvey say, "Now, I'm about to tell you a little more than I know."

You have heard and read many explanations of what the spirit, soul, and body are, but if you would indulge me a few minutes, I would like to submit mine. This is my view regarding our holistic human makeup identified here by the apostle Paul as "spirit and soul and body."

Remember I'm not trying to rewrite theology. I claim no special revelation in this area. This is nothing more than my own simple explanation of our make-up in terms of these three aspects of our being as created by God. I'm simply trying to bring some understanding about what goes on inside most all of us and why.

Before we look at the scriptures, my reason for writing this chapter is simply to explain why we sometimes experience inconsistencies in our own lives regarding our tendencies toward godly things and/or carnal things. Why do we struggle within ourselves regarding the things we *want* to do as opposed to the things we are *supposed* to do?

THE IMAGE OF GOD

We are told in scripture that we are created in the image of God.

> *So God created man in his own image, in the image of God created he him; male and female created he them.*
> *Genesis 1:27*

Just as we see three aspects of God in one being, we have three elements of our own being.

> *For in him [Jesus] dwelleth all the fulness of the Godhead bodily.*
> *Colossians 2:9*

Just as there is only one God, I am only one person. Yet within me it seems as though there is more than one area of influence, which is why, I believe, I am often conflicted. Paul wrote about it repeatedly and I will try to explain why he did.

Just as Jesus was a fusion of Spirit and flesh, we also are a fusion of spirit and flesh.

SPIRIT, SOUL, AND BODY DEFINED

Let's start with some very simple statements about each of these three elements of our make-up and how they explain the mysteries of how we function. The following descriptions have solved some of these mysteries regarding inner conflicts I've experienced as I attempt to live as a Christian in this world. For me, it explains how we can be both spiritual beings and fleshly, carnal beings.

The soul is who I am. It is my personality. It is the part of me that is uniquely me and no one else. It is the location of my will, my thoughts, my feelings, my personhood. It is simply who I am as distinguished from every other person who ever lived or ever will live. My soul is me.

The body is my flesh. It is the house that my soul lives in. It is the vehicle that gets me around in the world. It is my connection with the world around me. It is what people currently see and the image by which they know me.

The spirit is life. It is the part that comes directly from God. It is what animates my being, enables me to breathe, move, grow, and live. (This may be the part that differs from what others think, but I will attempt to give my rationale for this in a few moments.)

Let me expand a little on this.

THE SOUL

A few years ago a friend of mine named Bruce called me and told me that he was passing through the town where I lived and wondered if I might have time for a cup of coffee. Happily, I said yes and met him shortly thereafter.

Bruce and I had been close friends when we were in college nearly forty years prior. From that time, our lives took us in different directions, and we lost contact with each other, so I had not seen him in many years. As one might expect, time had rendered several changes in our physical appearance. I will refrain from describing the changes that had occurred in Bruce—suffice it to say that if we had passed each other on the street somewhere, I may not have recognized him. He most likely would have been a stranger to me. He may have thought the same things about me.

When we successfully identified one another in the restaurant parking lot, we went in and sat down. It was only a couple of minutes before I heard the familiar laugh, observed the familiar mannerisms, listened to the familiar way of talking, including some of his verbal expressions. It was unmistakably Bruce, and we just seemed to pick up where we had left off years before. We had a great visit reliving stories of years past and catching up with our current lives.

The point of this anecdote is that Bruce's flesh had changed, no question about that, but one aspect of this man was still the same. That is my view of the soul. It is who we are.

Regardless of the physical changes that happen to us along the journey from birth to old age, we continue to be the same person. Why? Because even though our physical appearance is constantly changing, it is our soul that really defines who we are, not just our bodies.

A Brief Pause for Clarification

In the course of this chapter as well as the next, I will be referring mostly to the flesh and the spirit while referring very little to the soul. For visualization purposes, consider the spirit on one side, the flesh on the other side, and the soul in the middle. The ultimate path that the soul (the individual, the person) travels will be determined by which side of the person gains preeminence—the spirit or the flesh. One could almost say that the soul can be caught in the middle of these occasional personal skirmishes. Ultimately, though, it is the soul that makes the final determination. As the psalmist said (119:109), "My soul is continually in my hand."

THE BODY

The body is simple to understand. We all know about the flesh because we deal with it every day. In our flesh we experience hunger, pain, fatigue, energy, pleasure. We are cold and shivering, hot and sweaty, and so on.

I have heard it said that the cell structure of our flesh is constantly changing so that every seven years or so we virtually have new bodies. Do you believe that? I don't know whether I do or not, but when I look in the mirror, I see that I have morphed into a combination of my father and my mother's father. Go figure.

As I said, the body is the physical house we live in, the vehicle that gets us from here to there. Our body is the physical expression of who we are, the first level of expression of ourselves to the world around us.

THE SPIRIT

My statements about this may conflict with the views of others, but my view is that the spirit is life itself. It is that which gives life to our body and soul. Even though it is not actually the Spirit of God, it truly does come *from* God.

Consider the account of the creation of Adam.

> *And the* Lord *God formed man of the dust of the ground, and breathed into his nostrils the breath of life; and man became a living soul.*
>
> Genesis 2:7

As God hovered over this newly created body, it lay motionless and lifeless until God's breath of life was breathed into its nostrils, and suddenly that body came alive. Man became a living soul. Adam's soul and Adam's body came alive when the breath of God entered into him.

So the flesh came from the dust of the earth while the spirit came from God.

> *Then shall the dust return to the earth as it was: and the spirit shall return unto God who gave it.*
> *Ecclesiastes 12:7*

It is my opinion that this *life* we are talking about is not the same as plant life or animal life. Most scientists think that life is life, whether it is a human being or moss on a rock. If the robot touring the planet Mars finds a patch of moss in a ditch, it will make news around the world. It will be announced on every network, in every newspaper, and all over the internet, that we have discovered life on Mars.

While that may truly be an amazing scientific discovery, it would not indicate much to me because I personally would not consider a patch of moss as being even remotely the same as the life that was introduced into Adam's nostrils by the breath of God.

To many, life is, well, just life. To me there is the functional, chemical, growing life of a plant or even an animal, and then there is human life. The two are very different!

THE CONFLICT

Regarding the conflict I mentioned a few paragraphs ago, most—if not all—of us experience inner conflict from time to time between the spirit and the flesh. The spirit is the part of me that comes from God. It is not mere animation; it is actually an element of life that has a unique connection to God from whom it comes, and that spirit truly longs for God and the things that pertain to him. On the other hand, the flesh longs for the things of the world such as comfort and pleasure and appeasements of various kinds.

The apostle Paul spoke of this conflict several times in various epistles. It was not just a small passing subject that Paul mentioned offhandedly; it was a major message of his writings. And it is a good thing because it is a universal problem about which we need spiritual understanding and guidance. I believe this conflict affects everyone.

I would love to announce to all who read this that I personally never experience inner conflict. I would love to claim such total unity between myself and God that I never experience doubt, fear, temptation, anger, or jealousy. (In the interest of my image, I think I'll stop there.) I think you get my meaning.

The truth is that all of us sometimes find ourselves pulled in multiple directions. The enemy never gives up in his attempt to draw us away from God. He has manufactured a plethora of enticements to send our way. We live in a sinful world, and its appeal to our flesh is the many pleasures it promises.

> *For what I am doing, I do not understand. For what I will to do, that I do not practice; but what I hate, that I do.*

> *If, then, I do what I will not to do, I agree with the law that it is good. But now, it is no longer I who do it, but sin that dwells in me.*
>
> *For I know that in me (that is, in my flesh) nothing good dwells; for to will is present with me, but how to perform what is good I do not find. For the good that I will to do, I do not do; but the evil I will not to do, that I practice.*
>
> Romans 7:15–19, NKJV

So what is Paul saying? He is telling us that he's not that much different from the rest of us. He apparently experienced the normal inner conflicts the rest of us mortals know so well.

What was the basis of that conflict? Paul identified it as the *sin that dwells in me*. If he had been delivered from sin, then where was the sin that he referred to? He said it was *in my flesh*. As we can see, the temptation to sin, even in the born-again Christian, is in that part of our existence that we know as the flesh.

A Brief Pause for a Personal Recollection

I remember a preacher who was very highly thought of in my denomination. He spoke at several conferences, camp meetings, and ministers' retreats, and conducted lots of seminars. He held several important positions of leadership and pastored several good churches. To many young ministers like me, he was a role model. He was literally one of my heroes. One time while speaking at a conference, he was asked to give some advice based upon his vast experience. To my surprise, he said he felt that the thing of which he was the best example was a struggle. A struggle? I would never have thought that, but his message to us was that life is never easy; there are no magic keys; the best advice would not automatically make you a success.

To me it appeared as though life was easy for him, but, according to him, it never was. Why? Because there were always personal issues of conflict that had to be dealt with. For instance, because he was regularly called upon to speak at conferences and seminars, he could have been tempted to be proud, arrogant, and self-sufficient. The spiritual side of the man says to stay humble; the carnal, fleshly side has other ideas. The spiritual side says, *Don't forget where you came from and the grace of God that has enabled you to get to where you are.* The fleshly side says, *Yes, I am amazing, that's for sure!*

Back to Paul

My view of the apostle Paul was that life must have been a breeze for him. After all, he was not just an ordinary man, was he. He was some sort of superman, one who knew nothing of inner conflict. He must have been so sure of himself and so balanced that he never struggled with anything. Not true, apparently.

The personal issues Paul dealt with are not specifically named. He simply spoke of the importance of walking in the Spirit as opposed to the flesh, assuring us that Jesus has made provisions for us regarding these human tendencies.

> *There is therefore now no condemnation to them which are in Christ Jesus, who walk not after the flesh, but after the Spirit. For the law of the Spirit of life in Christ Jesus hath made me free from the law of sin and death. For what the law could not do, in that it was weak*

through the flesh, God sending his own Son in the likeness of sinful flesh, and for sin, condemned sin in the flesh: That the righteousness of the law might be fulfilled in us, who walk not after the flesh, but after the Spirit.

For they that are after the flesh do mind the things of the flesh; but they that are after the Spirit the things of the Spirit. For to be carnally minded is death; but to be spiritually minded is life and peace. Because the carnal mind is enmity against God: for it is not subject to the law of God, neither indeed can be. So then they that are in the flesh cannot please God.

Romans 8:1–8

This I say then, Walk in the Spirit, and ye shall not fulfil the lust of the flesh. For the flesh lusteth against the Spirit, and the Spirit against the flesh: and these are contrary the one to the other: so that ye cannot do the things that ye would.

Galatians 5:16–17

I may not know what Paul's issues were, but I know what mine are. You probably know yours too. Let's be honest; there are temptations around every corner, and we may find ourselves drawn in directions that we know we shouldn't go. There are ways to deal with these issues and temptations. It is up to us to study the scripture diligently to find the teachings that help us to overcome in those areas of the spirit versus the flesh.

As we contend with the issues of our personal lives and the inner conflicts we often have, it may help to understand the way the two aspects of our lives—spirit and flesh—work. Maybe that understanding will be a step in gaining greater control of our personal lives.

~ Chapter 11 ~

WHAT ABOUT JESUS?

SPIRIT, SOUL, AND BODY CONTINUED

One of the points of this book is to show the great similarity in how the spirit world works and how the natural world works. The mirror image between the two is such that the natural world was used by Jesus to describe and explain the spiritual world.

In chapter 9, we looked at the dichotomy between the flesh and the spirit in people. It is the two sides of every person, the spirit side, which leans toward God, and the fleshly side, which tends to prefer the elements of the world.

Paul explained in Romans 7 that his inner struggle regarding what he should do and should not do was due to his flesh. He said, "For I know that in me (that is, in my flesh) dwelleth no good thing" (Romans 7:18). That sounds harsh, I know. But what did he mean? He meant that the flesh, simply left to its inclinations, would lead the person toward the world and not toward God.

Humans are a complex combination of spirit and flesh. Also in chapter 9, we looked at the Genesis account stating that we were created in the image of God. This brings us to Jesus Christ. The Bible tells us that he was "the image of God" (2 Corinthians 4:4). In another verse, it refers to him as "the image of the invisible God" (Colossians 1:15). In still another verse he is said to be "the express image of [God's] person" (Hebrews 1:3).

So, Jesus, who was "made like unto his brethren" (Hebrews 2:17), was also a fusion of Spirit and flesh. He was truly God and truly man. As Paul told Timothy, "God was manifest in the flesh" (1 Timothy 3:16).

GOD'S ENTRANCE INTO THE WORLD

Mary, a young Jewish virgin, was chosen as the one who would bring Jesus, the Son of God, into the world. An angel appeared to her to announce God's plan for her.

> *And the angel answered and said unto her, The Holy Ghost shall come upon thee, and the power of the Highest shall overshadow thee: therefore also that holy thing which shall be born of thee shall be called the Son of God.*
> Luke 1:35

Joseph was engaged to be married to Mary, but when he received word that she was expecting a child, he was greatly troubled, and understandably so. He was planning to quietly break the engagement when an angel appeared to him to explain this extraordinary development. He was told not to be afraid to take Mary as his wife because the child she was carrying was conceived by God. Following is the angelic message that explained how this child would be the fulfillment of an age-old prophecy.

> *Behold, a virgin shall be with child, and shall bring forth a son, and they shall call his name Emmanuel, which being interpreted is, God with us.*
> Matthew 1:23

I chose these verses to show how the birth of Jesus was indeed God taking on human flesh. We often use the phrase *when God became a man* to describe the phenomenon of the earthly existence of Jesus Christ. With this in mind, let me show you how Jesus bears out the explanation of spirit and flesh and how the conflict works in all of us.

WHY DID SATAN THINK HE COULD TEMPT JESUS?

I don't know about you, but I have trouble ascribing the same type of humanity to Jesus that I myself have, so I'm going to be very careful here. But do we not claim that while Jesus was fully God, he also was fully man? What does that mean with regard to his existence on this earth?

For instance, what was going on in the temptation immediately following his baptism?

If Jesus was truly tempted—and he was (See Hebrews 2:18, 4:15)—what did Satan assume to be the location of his weakness—the area in which he *could* be tempted? Obviously, the area upon which he focused was his flesh. It was on the basis of this perceived vulnerability that Satan planned three specific temptations, all of which were designed to appeal in some way to the flesh.

The First Temptation

"If thou be the son of God," Satan challenged, "command that these stones be made bread" (Matthew 4:3). After all, Jesus had been fasting for forty days and was extremely hungry. By doing what Satan suggested, he could accomplish two things: he could satisfy his hunger with much-needed food while simultaneously proving to Satan, and maybe even himself, that he was indeed the Son of God.

Maybe this was one of the reasons that at his baptism by John at the Jordan River the voice spoke from heaven declaring, "This is my beloved son in whom I am well pleased" (Matthew 3:17). As Jesus was driven into the wilderness immediately following that baptismal ceremony, he entered into that long period of fasting and isolation with the assurance that he truly was God's son. So he didn't need to reinforce that fact by allowing Satan to dictate anything to him. He was, at that moment, living by the very words that had proceeded out of the mouth of God forty days before.

The Second Temptation
The second temptation was to prove that the angels of heaven would rally to Jesus' rescue even if he were to cast himself off the pinnacle of the temple. That would have been an impressive spectacle! It would have shown how vitally important he was to the mission of heaven.

The Third Temptation
The third temptation had to do with Jesus falling prostrate before Satan, worshiping him. The reward for doing so, he was told, would be that he would immediately be set up as the owner of all the earth's kingdoms. A shortcut to glory!

Each of the three temptations was designed to appeal to the fleshly desires that Satan *thought* he could exploit in Jesus. Of course, we know that Jesus was more than able to resist Satan's advances, giving us the assurance that we also can resist similar temptations in our lives.

THE GARDEN OF GETHSEMANE

What about Jesus' prayer in the Garden of Gethsemane? This has always intrigued me. The prayer, "Not my will, but thine be done" (Luke 22:42), is an amazing revelation to me.

As we said before, in Jesus we see the fusion of God and man, of Spirit and flesh.

Some see one person in the Godhead speaking to another person in the Godhead, but I see it as a demonstration of the will of the flesh being different from the will of the Spirit.

When Jesus said to his disciples, "The spirit indeed is willing, but the flesh is weak" (Matthew 26:41), was he referring only to the inner conflict the disciples were dealing with? Or was he also giving us a glimpse into what he was experiencing?

Why would any fleshly being relish the horror that was about to be unleashed upon Jesus? Why would one who had been sinless and perfect want to drink of that detestable cup? What flesh would not shrink from the horrendous pain and unspeakable suffering that awaited Jesus? Was there no other way? Would it be possible for him to accomplish his mission by some other means? The whips, the thorns, the nails, the taunts, the rejection—what fleshly being would choose that?!

Jesus was God manifest in the flesh and his flesh seemed, on some level at least, to have some semblance of a will of its own.

I hope my caution is coming through in my presentation of Jesus that in a way we all could find offensive. Some may find it impossible to believe he could have struggled at all in this decision and believe me, I get that. Consider, however, the account of Luke, the beloved physician.

> *And he was withdrawn from them about a stone's cast, and kneeled down, and prayed, saying, Father, if thou be willing, remove this cup from me: nevertheless not my will, but thine, be done. And there appeared an angel unto him from heaven, strengthening him. And being in an agony he prayed more earnestly: and his sweat was as it were great drops of blood falling down to the ground.*
>
> Luke 22:41–44

A picture is presented of a man enjoined in an epic battle. This was not some placid, ritualistic prayer being offered as a formality before a religious ceremony. This was war. The battle was between the flesh and the Spirit. It was as though the flesh was crying out, *Please don't make me do this!* And yet in the course of this battle, the will of the flesh succumbed to the will of the Spirit as Jesus said, "Not my will, but thine be done."

Is this not a facsimile of the conflict that sometimes wages within us? While the stakes are not the same by any means, the inner conflict is still there. Our flesh pulls us one way; our spirit pulls us another way.

JESUS CHRIST, OUR PERFECT EXAMPLE

> *For to this you were called, because Christ also suffered for us, leaving us an example, that you should follow His steps.*
>
> 1 Peter 2:21, NKJV

> *For verily he took not on him the nature of angels; but he took on him the seed of Abraham. Wherefore*

> *in all things it behoved him to be made like unto his brethren, that he might be a merciful and faithful high priest in things pertaining to God, to make reconciliation for the sins of the people. For in that he himself hath suffered being tempted, he is able to [aid] them that are tempted.*
>
> Hebrews 2:16–18

For the sake of clarification, I hasten to say once again that *Jesus was not just like me.* He was God manifest in the flesh; I am just an ordinary man. His nature was divine; mine is anything *but* divine. What he did was to set an example for me—for all of us—of what it takes to be an overcomer. The message was that the victories he won over the enemy can, by *his* power, be won by us as well. He is always there to help us.

WHEN GOD CALLS A SINNER

Every Sunday thousands of church services are conducted in which evangelistic sermons are preached and altar calls are given. Many people in attendance who have never surrendered to the Lord are experiencing a conviction that pulls them in the direction of God. The invitation is given to come forward and a battle ensues. It's that battle between the flesh and the spirit. The spirit says to the soul, *Take me down to that altar*, while the flesh rebels against any such move. I have heard the conflict referred to as *white-knuckle resistance* (holding tightly to the back of the pew until the knuckles turn white). In some instances, the spirit wins out over the flesh and the person walks down the aisle and kneels before God at the altar. At other times, the flesh wins the battle, and the person leaves in the same spiritual condition in which he came. It happens.

SOME DO NOT STRUGGLE; THEY JUST GIVE IN

> *Now while Paul waited for them at Athens, his spirit was stirred in him, when he saw the city wholly given to idolatry.*
>
> *Acts 17:16*

As we look at this verse, two things jump out at me: first, the phrase that says "Paul's spirit was stirred in him"; second, the description of the city being "wholly given to idolatry." In just a few words we see Paul, who was motivated by his spiritual side, and those citizens of Athens, who were completely given to the fleshly pursuits of idolatry.

Having said this, it bears noting that Paul conveyed a very interesting observation in the following verse.

> *For as I passed by, and beheld your devotions, I found an altar with this inscription, TO THE UNKNOWN GOD. Whom therefore ye ignorantly worship, him declare I unto you.*
>
> *Acts 17:23*

It seemed that within this idolatrous city that was wholly given to cultural, religious practices that were, for the most part, motivated by sensuality and perversion, there existed a desire to know something different. Could it be they were admitting, albeit in a cryptic way, that despite all they had, or thought they had, there was a gnawing suspicion that there must be more? Something better? They seemed to be saying, *Surely, this is not all there is.*

Paul seemed to think so, because he seized upon that inscription TO THE UNKNOWN GOD to declare the one whom he thought they, at least on some spiritual level, hungered for.

Many people seem so totally given to carnal, fleshly pursuits that they apparently have no interest in God at all. I contend that in every such person there is a spiritual side which, if the opportunity ever arises, could awaken with a desire to know God. Regardless of how much a person is given to the world and all its pleasures, there is never a sense of true happiness apart from God. At least that's what I think.

IN CONCLUSION

In keeping with the title of this book, *That's Just the Way It Works*, let me state that the point of these two chapters on spirit, soul, and body is an attempt to give a plausible explanation about how and why we tend to struggle in life. Our inner conflicts regarding living righteously in a sensual, sinful world are natural. We should not despair when we experience these battles because everyone does. Paul did. I do, and so do you. God will, however, help us to be overcomers if we will put our faith and trust in him.

How does one do that? Well, consider this simple illustration I heard years ago. It is told in several different ways, but the basic message is the same.

An elderly Native American gentleman told his friend of the conflict that went on inside him, describing it by saying, "There are two wolves inside me, one good and one evil. They are always fighting."

The friend asked the gentleman, "Which one wins?"

The man replied, "The one I feed."

Walk in the spirit and mind the things of the spirit—these are the keys. Don't give place to fleshly pursuits. Nurture the spiritual side of life and it will be much easier to avoid the temptations that the flesh is naturally drawn to.

I hope that as we proceed you will come to understand more about how to tap into the wonderful blessings of God. The more we understand how it all works, the better able we'll be to claim those blessings in our lives.

~ Chapter 12 ~
BEING AN OVERCOMER

PART ONE: HOW DOES THAT WORK?

To him that overcometh will I grant to sit with me in my throne, even as I also overcame, and am set down with my Father in his throne.
Revelation 3:21

There are many principles in the Bible that can work just fine without us understanding how. Grace, for example, is an interesting aspect of God's work in our lives, but a detailed understanding of how grace works is not necessary for us to receive its benefits. One can be saved without knowing anything about grace, theologically speaking. Once saved, Christians can be strengthened and preserved in their walk with God, which is a function of grace, without being able to give a lengthy, detailed Bible study about the subject. Some things just work.

This chapter addresses something that can be a problem to many—that of overcoming temptations, addictions, or whatever we deal with on an ongoing basis that can be detrimental to our lives. Once again, it is not always necessary to have a thorough knowledge of how it works. One may do some of the things we will mention as instructed by a counselor. Some may even do them instinctively. It may, however, be easier if we understand how and why these things work.

Thus, the focus of this chapter is how we can be overcomers. Platitudes regarding various scriptural instructions often leave us wondering how they can be applied. The more we understand how things work, the more effectively we can put them into practice.

Temptation is universal to all humans. Someone humorously stated, *I can resist anything but temptation.* As funny as that may sound, we are seldom, if ever, tempted to do anything that would not on some level be pleasurable, desirable, or maybe even advantageous.

Temptation is not always attached to sinful activities. One can be tempted to do all sorts of things that will not lead one down an evil path. A man can be tempted to quit a good job to take a better one. A woman can be tempted to change her college major in favor of a different one. I can be tempted to eat a big piece of peach cobbler under a mound of ice cream in violation of my diet. In writing this book, I may be tempted to add or delete a chapter for one reason or another. (I am thinking of one right now.)

Thus, we can be tempted to do things, make choices, change our direction in some way, move to another house, buy a new car, or any number of other things that would not necessarily be harmful. Temptations like that most likely would not need to be overcome.

There are, however, things in life that we are tempted to do that may be harmful to us in many ways, including our spiritual lives. Several Bible verses deal with various aspects of our lives as we grapple with temptation and the efforts we put forth to overcome those temptations. Here is one.

> *For whatsoever is born of God overcometh the world:*
> *and this is the victory that overcometh the world, even*

> *our faith. Who is he that overcometh the world, but he that believeth that Jesus is the Son of God?*
>
> 1 John 5:4–5

In these verses we see the importance of faith. Faith is what enables us to access the help that comes from God. Our heartfelt belief that Jesus was not just an interesting prophet but truly the Son of God is paramount to us receiving the help that only he can give. And remember it was Jesus who stated in John 16:33, "I have overcome the world." Because of this, we know that by his help we can be overcomers also.

In previous chapters we spoke of issues involving flesh and spirit. We said that our flesh can be lured to go in one direction whereas our spirit can desire something else. (Please refer to chapters 9 and 10.) Our flesh can be tempted with things of the world that can take control of our lives and maybe even destroy us. Some of the obvious pitfalls can include alcohol, drugs, cigarettes, gambling, and pornography. These are some of the obvious things that many minds automatically go to, but they are by no means the only things that one might need to overcome.

Addictions to power, control, money, work, even hobbies and such like can get a firm hold on people, taking them in directions that would destroy their marriage, family, friendships, business, health, and maybe even their relationship with God. It not only *can* happen; it *does* happen.

As the scripture cited above says, "To him that overcomes will I grant to sit with me in my throne." This seems to promise an eternal reward for overcoming various types of temptations. We all have them, but temptations can vary from one person to another. One may be tempted with one thing, whereas another may have no inclination in that direction. Each of us, however, must understand that harmful thoughts, activities, desires, obsessions, and/or any number of other things that plague us need to be dealt with and overcome. Otherwise they can take hold of us, control us, and maybe even destroy us.

> *The thief cometh not, but for to steal, and to kill, and to destroy: I am come that they might have life, and that they might have it more abundantly.*
>
> *John 10:10*

Make no mistake, the thief, the enemy of our soul, the devil, would do anything to ensnare us in something that would drag us down, even destroy us. While Jesus' desire and plan for us is abundance of life, Satan's plan is for our destruction.

Though Satan cannot force us to do anything, he can watch us and observe the things we do or say and the places we go. This enables him to determine the areas of our vulnerabilities. He then will put those things in our path to entice us and lure us into his trap.

ALL WE LIKE SHEEP

The Bible often likens us to sheep. Isaiah 53:6 says, "All we like sheep have gone astray. We have turned every one to his own way."

What is the correlation? Apparently, sheep have very little sense of direction and can easily be drawn away from the flock to eat from a different clump of grass or clover. A sheep can wander from one area to another until it becomes lost, something it never would have anticipated. When the sheep realizes it has strayed, it becomes frightened because it cannot find its way back to the safety of the flock. This is when the sheep, which is virtually defenseless, is most vulnerable to being attacked and killed.

One of the realities of humanity is the tendency to wander like sheep. We are always looking for something else, something more exciting, interesting, or stimulating. Having something good does not mean we are not continually on the lookout for something better.

As James 1:14 tells us, "Every man is tempted, when he is drawn away of his own lust, and enticed." Lust is a powerful, inordinate desire. It could be for anything. At the risk of redundancy, I state one more time that Satan makes it his business to know, or at least to seek to know, what those things are for each of us. He then attempts to lure us away into his chosen direction and get us hooked or addicted to something that will eventually bring us down.

People are rarely fearful of addiction. They venture into areas that most anyone could know are dangerous, but do not think they will become addicted. Addiction is never the intended result of any kind of activity, but once they are "hooked," it is exceedingly difficult to overcome.

At times they deny there is a problem at all; they claim they can stop at any time because there is no addiction. Then there are those who do not want to overcome the addiction because they enjoy it too much. They are happily addicted and will readily admit it.

Not much can be done for people until they realize they have a problem and are motivated to do whatever is necessary to overcome it.

In the following paragraphs my intention is not to set forth *method* so much as *principle*. While one can do certain things to be an overcomer, some specific biblical principles apply to all who seek to be overcomers.

THE BLOOD OF THE LAMB AND OUR TESTIMONY

Earlier in the chapter, we looked at a verse from 1 John 5 regarding overcoming the world. Here is a passage in Revelation that addresses the same subject.

> *And I heard a loud voice saying in heaven, Now is come salvation, and strength, and the kingdom of our God, and the power of his Christ: for the accuser of our brethren is cast down, which accused them before our God day and night. And they overcame him by the blood of the Lamb, and by the word of their testimony; and they loved not their lives unto the death.*
>
> *Revelation 12:10–11*

These verses speak to us from the standpoint of our spiritual relationship with God as a person who has been born again. We know that Satan is forever our enemy, attempting to destroy us in any way possible. Verse 10 above refers to Satan as the accuser of the brethren and states that he accuses us day and night before God.

That reminds me of the account in the Old Testament book of Job where it states that on two different occasions Satan came to God accusing Job of serving God only because he pampered and protected him while enabling him to be the richest, most influential man in the area, maybe even the world. Satan challenged God to prove that Job was as good as God said he was. God, you remember, on both of those occasions (Job 1:8; 2:3), declared Job to be perfect and upright, stating that he feared God, and hated evil.

The story of Job is a fascinating one, but a bit too long for us to tell here. Suffice it to say that most of us would be quite surprised if God or anyone else referred to us as perfect. Even though you and I are far from perfect, we are considered by God to be so by the blood of Jesus. In a spiritual sense, we have had the precious blood of Jesus applied to our lives. When God looks at us, he sees not our imperfections, but that perfection imputed to us by the blood of Jesus, which has cleansed us from all sin.

Someday this accuser will be cast down and destroyed. In the meantime, however, when he approaches with his accusations and insidious plans to destroy us by his destructive temptations, we can *plead the blood*.

Plead the Blood?!

What does it mean to *plead the blood?* It means to declare to Satan, or anyone else who needs to hear it, that it is the blood of Jesus that has cleansed us, not we ourselves. We may have weaknesses, but we have been delivered from sin by the blood of Jesus. Our strength is in the power of his blood, his name, and our personal relationship with him. The purity, the power, and the perfection of Jesus Christ has been conferred upon us. So Satan is not coming against you or me; he is coming against the blood of Jesus Christ.

Overcome by the Word of Our Testimony?

What does *overcome by the word of our testimony* mean? I believe it refers to what we declare in terms of the grace, mercy, and forgiveness we received from our Lord. When we resist Satan by our testimony regarding the blood of Jesus Christ and what it has done for us, the enemy will flee from us. By this, we will overcome.

There is a difference between knowing something and confessing it; that is, acknowledging it verbally, vocally, out loud. Knowing it is one thing, but a verbal testimony makes it even more real, more powerful.

CONTINUING TO BE AN OVERCOMER

In the paragraphs above we spoke of the spiritual aspect of overcoming temptations. This has mostly to do with our initial experience with God and how, from the point at which we became born-again Christians, we know that we are new creatures in Jesus.

What we also must know is that when we are saved—born again—we will always have the wonderful memory of that day. Most of us can remember the day, the place, and those who were with us. It will be a continual reality to us. However, our walk with God is not a one-time experience relating only to the day we came to the Lord. It is about an ongoing journey through life. There will be trials, tribulations, mountains, and valleys. And make no mistake, there will be temptations, and they will have to be dealt with in real time.

FROM THE SPIRITUAL TO THE PRACTICAL

In this chapter we have looked at temptation and how to understand it and deal with it mainly on a spiritual level. In the next chapter, we will look more at the practical side of the issue, which also is scriptural.

Too often I have found that teachers present theories, leaving me saying, *Okay, so what am I supposed to do with this?*

Hopefully, the next chapter will provide some practical help in answering this question.

~ Chapter 13 ~

BEING AN OVERCOMER

PART TWO: A PRACTICAL APPROACH

NO MAGIC WANDS

What is about to be set forth is not some magic wand that can be waved, miraculously making things all better. My purpose in writing about how things work is not to present a how-to manual. It is not a book of directions to be followed, step by step, to solve all problems. It is rather a book by which I try to explain the way things work as designed by God from creation.

Here it is again, the text that was the initial inspiration for this book. I hope you don't mind reading it once more.

> *The* Lord *by wisdom hath founded the earth; by understanding hath he established the heavens. By his knowledge the depths are broken up, and the clouds drop down the dew.*
>
> Proverbs 3:19–20

God's creation, infused with his wisdom, understanding, and knowledge, works just as he intended it to work. Thus, situations we find ourselves in—whether good, bad, or indifferent—are invariably the result of how things work. Sometimes our problems are produced by what we do; sometimes we are victimized by what others around us do. Our lives are inextricably linked and intertwined with the lives of others.

In most cases our addictions or other things we need to overcome are not forced upon us by others but are the result of the choices we have made. Realizing this, we must take advantage of what we know in our efforts to be overcomers.

FIRST, WE NEED THE HELP OF GOD

God Is Greater Than Man

In Job 33:12, a brief statement is presented to which most of us would readily agree: "God is greater than man."

We deal with many situations in our lives, temptation and addiction being among them. Sooner or later we come to the realization that we are incapable of overcoming these challenges on our own. We need the help of someone greater than we are.

I am declaring that God, Jesus Christ, is the one who can and will help us in this desperate time of need. He will be there for us if we will turn to him.

David was the king of Israel, the most powerful man in the land. He was referred to as *a man after God's own heart* (See 1 Samuel 13:14; Acts 13:22). One would think David was so sufficient in holiness, righteousness, and strength that he would never find himself in a horrible sinful condition. After his sin with Bathsheba and the egregious decision to cover it up by ordering the death of Uriah, her husband, David found himself in a pitiful condition. (See 2 Samuel 11:1–17.) He knew that he was insufficient in himself. Only God could help him. "Have mercy upon me, O God," was David's cry, (Psalm 51:1).

Many occasions in our lives require help from a much higher source. That source is Jesus Christ. We too can utter the plea, *Have mercy upon me, O God*, knowing that God pays attention to prayers like that.

There are many promises of God's help in scripture. Here is one.

> *Fear thou not; for I am with thee: be not dismayed; for I am thy God: I will strengthen thee; yea, I will help thee; yea, I will uphold thee with the right hand of my righteousness.*
>
> Isaiah 41:10

God assures his people that he will always be available to them, giving them help in their time of need. All we need to do is call on him and he'll be there.

SECOND, WE NEED THE HELP OF OTHER PEOPLE

Instructions Regarding One Another

In addition to the help we receive from the Lord, he also intends for us to turn to one another for help in our weaknesses. Consider some verses that instruct us to forge relationships with people who can be of help to us in our struggles.

> *Two are better than one; because they have a good reward for their labour. For if they fall, the one will lift up his fellow: but woe to him that is alone when he falleth; for he hath not another to help him up. Again, if two lie together, then they have heat: but how can one be warm alone? And if one prevail against him,*

> *two shall withstand him; and a threefold cord is not quickly broken.*
>
> Ecclesiastes 4:9–12

> *For none of us liveth to himself, and no man dieth to himself.*
>
> Romans 14:7

> *Confess your faults one to another, and pray one for another, that ye may be healed. The effectual fervent prayer of a righteous man availeth much.*
>
> James 5:16

These verses and many others show how important it is to have the help, understanding, and support of others when we are struggling. In many cases those who help each other are fellow strugglers. One must always know that regardless of how resolute one may be in the desire to overcome some difficult habit, "falling off the wagon" is still possible.

Becoming accountable to one another, being honest, and calling on others for help in times of weakness or temptation are especially important. When one falls, the other, who may also have fallen at some time or another, is there, not with judgment or condemnation but understanding and encouragement. People need people, and when people are in one another's lives, there is protection and accountability.

One other positive benefit of being accountable to others is the lightening of the load that one can experience when personal, private, unconfessed temptation is acknowledged to a loving, understanding friend. Often, those who struggle with these issues don't want anyone to know. They hide their struggles to avoid embarrassment, or to keep from giving the impression that they are weak, or to preserve some carefully protected image of personal virtue.

We all know people who seem to have the perfect life, people who appear to have everything together with no apparent problems. These impressions can often be false because the person has so successfully hidden his or her true inner issues. This can result in great stress as the person attempts to carry the load of secret struggles alone. When he or she finally admits the struggle to a friend or counselor, there is great relief. It is as if a portion of the load has been shifted to the shoulders of another. Someone is now helping to carry the burden.

"ONE ANOTHER" PRINCIPLES EXAMINED

In the New Testament (KJV) we find the words *one another* forty-one times. Various actions or interactions are mentioned in conjunction with these two words, such as love, forgive, comfort, and edify, as well as many others. There also are warnings against betraying, offending, judging, and provoking one another. The point is that our lives are, as we said before, intricately intertwined with the lives of others. While it is possible for us to be thorns in one another's sides (at which time we are to *forbear one another*, or if you prefer, *put up with one another*), it is also possible for us to be the source of great help and inspiration to our fellow human beings.

One of the most important aspects of church life is the understanding of how relationships work in the function of the church and in our individual lives.

The message is clear. Overcoming temptation is important, but in many cases, quite difficult to do alone. God has designed his creation to work in a certain way, and one of the principles is that we need God. In addition to our unquestioned need for God, however, there also is our need for one another.

It is rewarding to us when we have a personal connection with the God of the universe and the Savior of the world, but it also is extremely rewarding to have personal relationships with other people.

We cannot go it alone, and the beautiful truth is *we don't have to.*

LOVING GOD, LOVING PEOPLE

Relationships are central to our lives. Relationships with God and with people are both important. God has instituted his church in such a way as to make relationship with him to be seen in the context of relationships with his people.

Many years ago as a young minister attempting to start a church, I was knocking on doors and inviting people to attend our church services. One man opened one of those doors, and I extended my invitation. His response was that he didn't need to attend a church. His words are still firmly etched in my memory these many years since: "Me and Jesus, we have our own thing going." I took that statement to mean that his relationship was with Jesus alone and he didn't need people to be a part of that relationship. While I have no interest in judging the man's eternal soul based on his claim, it does remind me that in scripture we are told that our relationship with God is lived out in the context of our relationships with one another.

> *If someone says, "I love God," and hates his brother, he is a liar; for he who does not love his brother whom he*

> *has seen, how can he love God whom he has not seen?*
> *And this commandment we have from Him: that he*
> *who loves God must love his brother also.*
> 1 John 4:20–21, NKJV

When we love God, we tend to love the things that he loves. We want our interests to be the same as his. John tells us that "God is love" (1 John 4:8,16). He came to this earth to die for us because of his great love for us. If we claim to love him but not others for whom he died, we have missed one of the main points of his church. Our love for God is, in fact, demonstrated by virtue of our love for each other.

> *By this shall all men know that ye are my disciples, if*
> *ye have love one to another.*
> John 13:35

THE RISK OF ASKING FOR HELP

> *Brethren, if a man be overtaken in a fault, ye which are*
> *spiritual, restore such an one in the spirit of meekness;*
> *considering thyself, lest thou also be tempted. Bear ye*
> *one another's burdens, and so fulfil the law of Christ.*
> Galatians 6:1–2

Unfortunately, there are times when a person experiences a moral failure, addiction, weakness, or some other personal issue that would require someone else's help, but there is a reluctance to say anything to anyone. The reason for a person's hesitancy may be the fear of finding condemnation and isolation instead of help.

Some people relish the idea of knowing about the faults of the weak brother or sister, giving them the opportunity to compare themselves favorably with the struggler.

This is reminiscent of the woman accused of adultery being brought to Jesus by a group of Pharisees who wanted her to be made a public spectacle of immorality. Jesus made it clear that the punishment her accusers demanded must be initiated by the one who considered himself to be faultless.

The verse above instructs all of us who deem ourselves to be spiritual to receive the struggling person "in the spirit of meekness," realizing that sometime in the future, that weak person may be us.

The church is a fellowship. I know of a man who many years ago was asked to define the term *fellowship*. After a brief consideration of the request, he answered, *All the fellows in the same ship*. I like that. The truth is we are all in this together. The big-I-little-you mentality must be set aside.

No one is so holy and righteous that they are qualified to disregard the needs of others. When people need you or me to help them in overcoming the troubling issues of their lives, we should do our best to be there for them. They need prayer, encouragement, understanding, mercy, and confidentiality, and it's our responsibility to give it. It's the scriptural way.

SO...

Overcoming problems like addiction is neither simple nor easy. It can be a very long process of trying, failing, and trying again and again. It takes large amounts of desire, patience, and persistence.

I understand this subject cannot be covered comprehensively in two chapters of a book like this. What we are talking about is some very basic, rudimentary principles that can be helpful in this often-arduous process.

With this understanding, we are simply stating that a significant factor in being an overcomer is about our relationships with God and people. Availing ourselves of the help from God, the church, and its people will help us to be overcomers in this life and to be rewarded wonderfully in the life to come.

So, in essence, we need God, we need people, and people need us. And, yes, God has ordained it to work that way.

~ Chapter 14 ~

PROMISE OR PRINCIPLE?

The Bible Is Not a Book of One-Liners

Be diligent to present yourself approved to God, a worker who does not need to be ashamed, rightly dividing the word of truth.
2 Timothy 2:15, NKJV

Knowing this first, that no prophecy of the scripture is of any private interpretation.
2 Peter 1:20

We all like finding single verses from the scripture that give us inspiration, encouragement, and hope. Many people sign up to receive Verse of the Day messages on their email or text message accounts. Personally, I also like reading them. They can be uplifting and faith-building.

So, What Is a One-Liner?

Recently, while considering the interpretation of some specific Bible verses, the term "one-liner" occurred to me. Let me explain—there are comedians who are known for their use of one-liners—jokes that have no backstory to set up the punchline but are simply one or two short sentences. They are deemed to be self-explanatory and funny without further elaboration. But although one-liners can be funny, they also are usually silly, so please forgive me for not giving an example. Let me emphasize—Bible verses are not jokes. My point, however, is that while single verses, taken by themselves, may inspire hope and encouragement, they may need to be connected to several other verses to be fully understood.

GETTING BACK TO THE POINT

The mistake is sometimes made of choosing one verse and using it as a proof text on which to establish a Bible doctrine. While every verse is true and divinely inspired, each one must be interpreted correctly in the light of the rest of the Bible.

The verses above give us some insight into principles of Bible interpretation. The first one speaks of rightly dividing the word of truth. Without attempting to give a lengthy explanation of what that means, suffice it to say that the best interpreter of scripture is scripture itself. Rightly dividing the word may involve taking one verse, setting it aside, finding other verses that speak about the same subject, and placing them all side-by-side until we arrive at an understanding of what they all mean together.

The next verse tells us that no verse is of any private interpretation. The word *private* can signify being set apart from the rest, secluded, alone. The Amplified Bible states it this way: "No prophecy of Scripture is a matter of or comes from one's own [personal or special] interpretation." It seems to be saying that the interpretation of a single verse must not be arrived at to the exclusion of other verses that can add additional clarity.

May I suggest that these verses tell us that *the Bible is not a book of one-liners*. It is not to be interpreted privately, by one person, or apart from the rest of the verses on that subject. It is to be understood in the light of the entire Bible.

Many years ago I was taught that a general truth is interwoven throughout the scripture and that no single verse of scripture will ever contradict that general truth. When one verse seems to say something that differs from the general truth, it must be examined in context with the rest of the Bible.

This is one way of preventing us from arriving at erroneous doctrinal beliefs and/or fanciful conclusions regarding the promises of the Bible.

HAVING SAID ALL OF THAT...

The purpose of this chapter "Promise or Principle?" is to explain some verses that can seem to say something that may not be intended, at least without some qualification. People can read some very well-known verses and be discouraged because, based upon those individual verses, they expect things to work in a particular way, only to find out that they may not work as they think they should.

LIKE WHAT?

Well, like the verses regarding *asking, seeking, and knocking*.

(While there are several other subject areas in scripture that could be a part of this discussion, this is the one I'm most concerned about regarding the subject of this book.)

Here is a passage that needs to be understood as a "principle" as well as a "promise."

> *Ask, and it shall be given you; seek, and ye shall find; knock, and it shall be opened unto you: For every one*

> *that asketh receiveth; and he that seeketh findeth; and to him that knocketh it shall be opened.*
>
> *Matthew 7:7–8*

I'm not going to hedge on this; it does look like a promise—almost like a blank check. Here is another verse that can also be taken in this way.

> *And whatsoever ye shall ask in my name, that will I do, that the Father may be glorified in the Son. If ye shall ask any thing in my name, I will do it.*
>
> *John 14:13–14*

Believe me, it is definitely *not* my desire to diminish the power of prayer or the miraculous answers we often receive. But what happens when a person thinks this promise is broken when he or she asks for something specific and does not receive it?

Some people have adopted the "name it and claim it" notion regarding verses like those above. The impression given by this position is that if you have enough faith, you can literally name and claim anything you want.

I have often jokingly declared that if that were the case, I would be six feet three, weigh 195 pounds, and have a full head of hair—none of it gray. You may add to that a fancy red, very expensive sports car. I'm just saying . . .

So are verses such as those to be considered promises? The short answer is yes, but they, nonetheless, are verses that must be understood in the context of other verses regarding prayer and specific requests.

God wants us to pray, seek, and knock, but here is where we must understand the "principle" aspect of these verses as opposed to the absolute promise.

PRINCIPLES

If You Want to Receive, You Must Ask

Many years ago I attempted to make a living selling insurance. One day when I was very new at the job, my district manager rode with me to see how I was doing and to give me some pointers to help me to succeed. I remember him saying something like this: *Ron, don't be afraid to ask for the business, because, chances are, if you don't ask, you will not get the sale.* That is true, but I had to understand that in some cases I would ask but not get the sale. The lesson is that asking is necessary. If you want to receive, ask.

If You Want to Find, You Must Seek

As a parent, has your child ever told you that he or she cannot find something? *Did you look for it?* you might ask. *No*, the child answers. *Well, look for it*, you say.

Personally, I hate losing things, even insignificant things. When I lose something, I look for it. I mean hunt and search and seek for it, okay? Sometimes I look again and again, even in the same places. A bit obsessive, you might say. Well, maybe a little.

One thing is true: if you want to find something, you must seek for it. You may not find everything you seek for, but you will not find it unless you do.

If You Desire to Gain Entrance, You Must Knock

Knock; that is, pursue entrance into new areas of endeavor and blessing.

Back to my insurance-selling days. Sometimes I would go to a door a bit reluctantly, often hoping no one was home. I knew one thing, though. Once I arrived, I could not just stand there and hope someone inside would see me and come to the door. I had to knock.

Sometimes I knocked and no one came. Maybe they weren't home, or maybe they just didn't want to answer the door when they saw me standing there with my briefcase. Knocking, however, was a requirement if I wanted someone to answer the door.

So . . .

Asking, seeking, or knocking will never guarantee that you get everything you're hoping for. Not doing any of those things, however, will prevent you from getting any of them.

PROMISES

Keeping in mind how I've differentiated between *promises* and *principles*, I have chosen several verses, all of which can be claimed as promises because they are always true. We can be confident of each one, knowing it can be claimed whenever the need presents itself. Although I've listed only a few, there are many others that could be included.

Please remember I am in no way attempting to claim we cannot pray for and receive amazing answers to prayers for things that are not specifically promised. I believe in the power of prayer and the idea that "prayer changes things." The following verses contain some specific promises. Later, I will direct our attention to verses extolling the power of prayer.

> *God is our refuge and strength, a very present help in trouble.*
>
> Psalm 46:1

> *Fear thou not; for I am with thee: be not dismayed; for I am thy God: I will strengthen thee; yea, I will help thee; yea, I will uphold thee with the right hand of my righteousness.*
>
> Isaiah 41:10

> *Lo, I am with you alway, even unto the end of the world. Amen.*
>
> Matthew 28:20

> *Let your conversation be without covetousness; and be content with such things as ye have: for he hath said, I will never leave thee, nor forsake thee.*
>
> Hebrews 13:5

> *In my Father's house are many mansions: if it were not so, I would have told you. I go to prepare a place for you. And if I go and prepare a place for you, I will come again, and receive you unto myself; that where I am, there ye may be also.*
>
> John 14:2–3

> *Ye men of Galilee, why stand ye gazing up into heaven? this same Jesus, which is taken up from you into heaven, shall so come in like manner as ye have seen him go into heaven.*
>
> Acts 1:11

All of these verses contain promises that we can claim and cling to, knowing they are absolutely true.

PRAYER DOES CHANGE THINGS

Make no mistake about it, the Bible assures us that there's power in prayer. We are encouraged to pray about everything. When you are sick, discouraged, confused, burdened, or afraid, you are invited to bring your needs, physical and emotional, to the Lord in prayer knowing he will hear and answer.

The principle is that we are to pray. Nothing we pray about is out of bounds. God loves it when we pray, when we pour our hearts out to him. He wants us to share our deepest thoughts and concerns with him. There will always be an answer. God's will, however, is the most important aspect of answered prayers, and we must be mature enough as Christians to grasp that.

These verses are just a sampling of the many that speak of the power of prayer.

> *Now to Him who is able to do exceedingly abundantly above all that we ask or think, according to the power that works in us, to Him be glory in the church by Christ Jesus to all generations, forever and ever. Amen.*
>
> Ephesians 3:20–21, NKJV

> *Be careful for nothing; but in every thing by prayer and supplication with thanksgiving let your requests be made known unto God. And the peace of God, which passeth all understanding, shall keep your hearts and minds through Christ Jesus.*
>
> *Philippians 4:6–7*

> *Is any among you afflicted? let him pray. Is any merry? let him sing psalms. Is any sick among you? let him call for the elders of the church; and let them pray over him, anointing him with oil in the name of the Lord: And the prayer of faith shall save the sick, and the Lord shall raise him up; and if he have committed sins, they shall be forgiven him. Confess your faults one to another, and pray one for another, that ye may be healed. The effectual fervent prayer of a righteous man availeth much.*
>
> *James 5:13–16*

It is God's will that we all pray. Prayer is communication with him. It connects us to him and enables our faith to grow as we see what a difference prayer makes in our lives. It is not always about specific answers to our requests; it is more about our relationship and closeness with him.

> *O thou that hearest prayer, unto thee shall all flesh come.*
> *Psalm 65:2*

When we come to God in prayer, we need not come hat in hand, apologizing for taking up his time. We need not wonder, as

Esther did when she approached King Ahasuerus in that familiar Old Testament story (See Esther 4:11, 5:1-2), whether God will extend his scepter of acceptance to us. Will he be in a receptive mood, or will he turn from us and refuse to hear? The answer is that he will always receive us and listen intently to our supplication.

> *Let us therefore come boldly unto the throne of grace, that we may obtain mercy, and find grace to help in time of need.*
>
> *Hebrews 4:16*

As we consider the verses quoted earlier in this chapter regarding asking, seeking, and knocking, it is incumbent upon us all to remember that sometimes the things for which we ask may not be the will of God for us. God's plan for our lives is not always clear to us.

God is not just our partner; he is our Lord and Master. His plans are loftier and more wide ranging than ours tend to be. We cannot know everything he knows. That is why we should first ask for God's will to be done in our lives.

In addition to the idea of God being our Lord and Master, he also is to be acknowledged as our Father. "Our Father which art in Heaven" is how Jesus instructs us to pray in what has been called The Lord's Prayer (Matthew 6:9-13). As any good father would do, God hears our requests and evaluates them in terms of what is best for his child. What good father would give his children anything and everything they want? In today's world, that would be considered by many as tantamount to child abuse. While we do not compare God to good earthly fathers to determine what God should do, we simply put forth this observation to express that God will always have our best interests in mind as he receives our prayer requests and determines how they should be answered.

> *And this is the confidence that we have in him, that, if we ask any thing according to his will, he heareth us: And if we know that he hear us, whatsoever we ask, we know that we have the petitions that we desired of him.*
> *1 John 5:14–15*

In referencing the Lord's Prayer once again, we take note of the words "Thy will be done on earth as it is in heaven." This is one more indication that our prayers, which can and should be specific in what we desire from him, should also be coupled with our desire for the will of God to be done.

Even Jesus, in the Garden of Gethsemane, asked three times, "If it be possible, let this cup pass from me." But he concluded these requests with "nevertheless, not as I will, but as thou wilt" (Matthew 26:39-44).

THAT'S JUST A COP-OUT, SOME MAY SAY

Meaning what? Well, meaning that some might think I'm making excuses for all the "unanswered prayers" that people offer.

Some people think that when they pray for something and do not receive what they prayed for, they simply do not have enough faith—or that something is wrong with their prayer. Conversely, others assume that prayer is always a waste of time since, in their opinion, there is no God who is interested in anyone's prayers. Their assumption is that prayer is nothing more than a crutch anyway.

I have seen some amazing answers to prayer just as many of you readers have. Some of them were my prayers; others were the prayers of others. We know the power of prayer, and so we believe strongly in it. So asking that God's will be done is not a cop-out; it is simply an effort to put the principle of prayer into scriptural perspective so we have a mature understanding of what is *promise* and what is *principle*.

IN CONCLUSION

Prayer is not like coming up to the counter at a fast-food restaurant, placing your order, and receiving exactly what you ordered. But you know that.

Prayer is personal communication, communion, and conversation with God, our heavenly Father. It should include specific requests for things we need, and even things we want. There's nothing wrong with that. God loves it when we pray in accordance with his will, and he always answers.

~ Chapter 15 ~

WISDOM ALONE IS NOT ENOUGH

And God gave Solomon wisdom and understanding exceeding much, and largeness of heart, even as the sand that is on the sea shore. And Solomon's wisdom excelled the wisdom of all the children of the east country, and all the wisdom of Egypt. For he was wiser than all men . . . and his fame was in all nations round about.
1 Kings 4:29–31

So king Solomon exceeded all the kings of the earth for riches and for wisdom. And all the earth sought to Solomon, to hear his wisdom, which God had put in his heart.
1 Kings 10:23–24

It is well established that Solomon is considered the wisest natural man who ever lived. His wisdom, however, was not innate; it was given as a special gift from God himself. In chapter 2, we looked at the story of Solomon, his prayer, and God's very generous answer. God appeared to Solomon in a dream and asked what things he desired from God. Solomon asked that he be granted wisdom to be able to lead the people of Israel. God, commending him for his selfless request, granted him the gift of wisdom and much more.

It would be easy to assume that a man so gifted with wisdom would live a life that is wholesome and righteous, a life commensurate with the very principles that he himself set forth. Solomon's life, one would think, would be nearly perfect. Every choice would be a good choice, a wise choice. Unfortunately, that was not the case. Even though Solomon was exceedingly blessed with these gifts from God, his life took some very sad turns.

A SOBERING REMINDER FROM THE NEW TESTAMENT

I'm reminded of where Paul warned us "not to think of [ourselves] more highly than [we] ought to think" (Romans 12:3).

> *For who maketh thee to differ from another? and what hast thou that thou didst not receive? now if thou didst receive it, why dost thou glory, as if thou hadst not received it?*
>
> 1 Corinthians 4:7

Several years ago I stood before my congregation and bragged about the suit I was wearing. I told them what brand name was on the label, and everyone knew it indicated the suit was classy. I said I doubted that anyone else in the congregation had anything like it, indicating that I may be considered a notch above those who were unable to afford a suit like I was wearing.

As soon as I felt my point was well conveyed, I revealed to them that the suit had been purchased at a thrift store by a friend of mine only to find that it was too small for him. It fit me perfectly, so he asked me if I would like to have it. I said yes.

The point was and still is, *Don't brag about owning something that was given to you.*

The "designer" suit I wore that day said basically nothing about me. I wouldn't have had it if it had not been given to me.

It Was Just Given to You
God has given each one of us gifts of various kinds. You may have received a gift of public speaking, a beautiful singing voice, or the ability to play various musical instruments. You may have been blessed with a high level of intelligence or leadership skills or amazing physical beauty. The list could go on, but you know what I'm saying.

Whatever gift you possess that enables you to be front and center is not to be boasted of. It should not make you feel better than others around you. It was just given to you.

My silly story about the suit was simply to illustrate what Paul was saying in the verses above. Don't be so proud of who you are, what you are, what you have, or what you can do. Whatever special talents and abilities you have were just given to you. Use them thankfully. Use them to bless and benefit others. When you are done, realize that you are just another child of God like everyone else.

If you want to glorify anyone, glorify the one who gave you the gift—God.

SOLOMON KNEW THIS

> *Then I saw that wisdom excelleth folly, as far as light excelleth darkness. The wise man's eyes are in his head; but the fool walketh in darkness: and I myself perceived also that one event happeneth to them all. Then said I in my heart, As it happeneth to the fool, so it happeneth even to me; and why was I then more wise? Then I said in my heart, that this also is vanity. For there is no remembrance of the wise more than of the fool for ever;*

> *seeing that which now is in the days to come shall all be forgotten. And how dieth the wise man? as the fool.*
> *Ecclesiastes 2:13–16*

We see in Solomon's writings that he understood that having wisdom such as his didn't make him, in essence, different from any other man. Having such high levels of wisdom did not mean he was better than others. The wise man and the foolish man die just like everyone else. While it is better to be wise than foolish, there remains one event that no one escapes. Death is the great equalizer. It comes for us all.

Solomon's Cynicism

Solomon was a very complex man. It appears that his great wisdom caused him to become a bit cynical. He stated several times that everything was "vanity and vexation of spirit," adding in one place, "I hated life" (Ecclesiastes 2:17).

Solomon's wisdom was quite beneficial in making him a great king; but, according to him, it became a heavy burden. This, I believe, was the basis for some of the cynicism expressed in the book of Ecclesiastes as we read in the verses above. Solomon went on to say:

> *And I gave my heart to know wisdom, and to know madness and folly: I perceived that this also is vexation of spirit. For in much wisdom is much grief: and he that increaseth knowledge increaseth sorrow.*
> *Ecclesiastes 1:17–18*

The burden of Solomon's great wisdom wore him down to the place where he began to violate the very word of God, some of which he wrote.

Before Israel even had a king, they were warned about the pitfalls of setting a man up to be king over their nation. If they did it anyway, they were told, they should not choose a stranger, someone who was not an Israelite, to be a king. Also, warning was given to whomever would be afforded such an honor not to enrich himself greatly or lead the people into the ways of the world. The last part of the warning contained in the verses below had to do with the temptation to take on many wives, especially any who would turn the king's heart from serving God.

Here is the passage that states these instructions.

> *When thou art come unto the land which the LORD thy God giveth thee, and shalt possess it, and shalt dwell therein, and shalt say, I will set a king over me, like as all the nations that are about me; Thou shalt in any wise set him king over thee, whom the LORD thy God shall choose: one from among thy brethren shalt thou set king over thee: thou mayest not set a stranger over thee, which is not thy brother. But he shall not multiply horses to himself, nor cause the people to return to Egypt, to the end that he should multiply horses: forasmuch as the LORD hath said unto you, Ye shall henceforth return no more that way. Neither shall he multiply wives to himself, that his heart turn not away: neither shall he greatly multiply to himself silver and gold.*
>
> *Deuteronomy 17:14–17*

Sadly, as we will see later, Solomon violated everything written in the verses above. Could it be that Solomon's great wisdom and knowledge caused him to feel as though he was exempt from the rules and laws set forth by God? Or maybe he became weary of it all because he was world renowned for his great wisdom and was consulted and leaned upon by many people, both from his own kingdom and from people who came to him from far and wide. As he states in Ecclesiastes 1:18, "In much wisdom is much grief."

Solomon also told us of the dangers of thinking we are sufficient in our own understanding to chart our own paths. We can easily assume that our intellect, our education, and our good sense are quite enough to enable us to make our own decisions without leaning on the arm of God. The following verses, written by Solomon, show us that he knew this.

> *Trust in the* L<small>ORD</small> *with all thine heart; and lean not unto thine own understanding. In all thy ways acknowledge him, and he shall direct thy paths. Be not wise in thine own eyes: fear the* L<small>ORD</small>, *and depart from evil.*
>
> Proverbs 3:5–7

A Brief Pause for Perspective

Let's go back for just a moment to the place where Solomon said, "I hated life." That's quite an interesting comment made by the man who literally had everything. Riches and the lavish lifestyles they afford are never a guarantee of happiness and fulfillment. It certainly was not with Solomon.

Recently, as I was reading the book of Job, I came across some interesting verses that reminded me of Solomon's declaration that he hated life. Job said something similar. In Job 9 and 10 Job expresses his grief in words such as these: "I despise my life" (9:21 NKJV), "My soul is weary of my life" (10:1)," why did you bring me forth from the womb?...It would have been better for me if I would have been carried from the womb to the grave" (10:18-19 Author's Paraphrase).

So, just as Solomon hated life, Job also hated life, but their reasons were quite different.

My question is, *How could Job **not** feel as he did?* He was in excruciating pain—physical and emotional—and he had no idea why.

Here is a bit of pastoral encouragement. Jesus is never offended by our humanity. We feel things; we say things. Sometimes we say things in pain, fear, confusion, frustration, or impatience. Believe me when I say that Jesus understands. He is not hurt, insulted, put off, or upset. He gets it. Don't get me wrong; I'm not saying that some of the things we may say are fine, just understandable.

The good thing about Job's complaint is that even though he spoke out of great pain and confusion, he still was able to say, "Though he slay me, yet will I trust him" (Job 13:15).

You may be struggling with your situation. That's understandable. Many of us do at some point. Just don't discard your faith.

Solomon Did Not Practice What He Preached

> *But king Solomon loved many strange women, together with the daughter of Pharaoh, women of the Moabites, Ammonites, Edomites, Zidonians, and Hittites; Of the nations concerning which the Lord said unto the children of Israel, Ye shall not go in to them, neither shall*

> *they come in unto you: for surely they will turn away your heart after their gods: Solomon clave unto these in love. And he had seven hundred wives, princesses, and three hundred concubines: and his wives turned away his heart. For it came to pass, when Solomon was old, that his wives turned away his heart after other gods: and his heart was not perfect with the LORD his God, as was the heart of David his father.*
>
> 1 Kings 11:1–4

Solomon's wisdom, though amazing, was not enough to prevent him from making some egregious mistakes later in life. He accomplished some incredible things, not the least of which was the building of the majestic, ornate temple that he dedicated to God.

There is much to learn from Solomon. The wisdom he set forth in the books of Proverbs and Ecclesiastes is still revered today. So much understanding of life can be gleaned from his words. But there also is much to be learned from Solomon's downfall.

In the next chapter, I will attempt to analyze Solomon's life in such a way as to illuminate the lessons we all can learn from what ultimately became of Solomon and why.

For now, let us remember that even though this book is written for the purpose of helping us to understand how life tends to work, it is not in any way for the purpose of substituting wisdom for total dependence upon God. Believe me, we will never get to that point.

~ Chapter 16 ~
ONLY BY THE GRACE OF GOD

"Wisdom alone is not enough." That was the declaration of the last chapter in which we spoke of the amazing wisdom of Solomon in conjunction with his monumental failures.

Consider the sad irony of Solomon's life. God graciously answered his prayer for the wisdom that he felt he lacked. Feeling inadequate, he expressed his fear that he would not know what to do as king. He feared he would be incapable of leading Israel effectively. The remarkable gift of wisdom God bestowed upon him enabled him to lead the people of God. Unfortunately, his poor stewardship of that gift, along with the extra blessings that were given beyond his original request, proved to be the catalyst for his tragic downfall that ultimately resulted in the division of the kingdom.

Here are some verses that provide details of these events.

> *But king Solomon loved many strange women, together with the daughter of Pharaoh, women of the Moabites, Ammonites, Edomites, Zidonians, and Hittites . . . For it came to pass, when Solomon was old, that his wives turned away his heart after other gods: and his heart was not perfect with the* Lord *his God, as was the heart of David his father . . . And Solomon did evil in the sight of the* Lord, *and went not fully after the* Lord, *as did David his father . . . And the* Lord

> *was angry with Solomon, because his heart was turned from the* LORD *God of Israel, which had appeared unto him twice . . . Wherefore the* LORD *said unto Solomon, Forasmuch as this is done of thee, and thou hast not kept my covenant and my statutes, which I have commanded thee, I will surely rend the kingdom from thee, and will give it to thy servant.*
> 1 Kings 11:1,4,6,9,11

So begins the undoing of one of the greatest, wisest men who ever lived. Despite the generous gifts God gave to Solomon, not the least of which was this astounding wisdom that mystified the world, the latter portion of Solomon's life was a great disappointment. One may have thought that by virtue of the wisdom Solomon had been granted, he would have been quite capable of managing the extra blessings that were given to him, which included immense riches. Unfortunately, that did not prove to be the case.

In this chapter, I would like to speak of the need we all have that goes beyond great knowledge, understanding, and wisdom. It is the need for God and his grace.

I previously quoted the following verse and wrote a chapter about our need for wisdom, but here it is again.

> *Wisdom is the principal thing; therefore get wisdom: and with all thy getting get understanding.*
> Proverbs 4:7

Get wisdom, yes, but also seek to understand the purpose of wisdom. Wisdom is no substitute for reliance upon God and his grace. In fact, wisdom, if it is not viewed in proper context with one's humanity, can cause a person to feel self-sufficient and not really in need of God.

Knowledge, understanding, and wisdom—all are important for us to seek, but when we attempt to understand how our relationship with God really works, it is good to have additional help.

SO HOW *DOES* IT REALLY WORK?

I don't know how many rules I am breaking as I write this book. Probably quite a few (I even know what many of them are), but I'm simply trying in my own way to write about the simple, practical realities of living the Christian life.

It is good for us to know the word of God. Being able to explain the fundamental doctrines of the Christian church is important. Using the word of God skillfully is a great benefit to anyone.

In the Old Testament book of Hosea (4:6) we read, "My people are destroyed for lack of knowledge." It is my fear that many Christians in our churches know precious little about the Bible and think that what one *believes* is important, not necessarily what one *knows*.

With that in mind, even if you believe many of the basics of what I have endeavored to cite in this book, there is much more to living a fruitful Christian life than just knowing how it all works. Further, if you know the Bible backward and forward and can teach it and preach it with skill and authority, even that is not enough.

For the next few paragraphs, I would like to look at the apostle Paul's life.

SAUL OF TARSUS

This man was a fierce enemy of Jesus and the church. It was his mission to destroy it all, and he was not particular about how he went about it.

The story of Saul of Tarsus, who later became known as Paul, is much too long to tell here. Suffice it to say that it was on "the road to Damascus" where Jesus appeared to this murderous man, struck him down, and called him to follow a completely different path.

That deadly journey to Damascus ended not with Christians dying or being dragged back to Jerusalem for trial, but with the miraculous conversion of Saul of Tarsus, who ultimately and astoundingly became an apostle of Jesus Christ as well as a prolific contributor to the writings of the New Testament.

Over the next few years, the apostle Paul was blessed to receive some of the most amazing revelations any one man ever had. He was transported to a heavenly place and shown things that defy any description earthly words can afford.

Even though he was a Jew, firmly rooted in Mosaic Law and pharisaical adherence to that law, Jesus revealed to him a completely new understanding of heavenly kingdom law in the dispensation of grace. While Paul was not the only one to whom Jesus revealed his truth, he was the one chosen to set forth a major share of New Testament doctrines.

PLEADING WITH GOD FOR A PERSONAL MIRACLE

As blessed as Paul was, something in his life was quite bothersome to him. On three separate occasions he implored God to relieve him of this problem, which he referred to as "a thorn in the flesh."

I doubt that Paul approached God these three times with a casual "prayer request" submitted in the midweek prayer meeting. It very well may have been three separate focused efforts that included fasting and prayer, possibly in a secluded place for several days. He desperately wanted to be rid of this "thorn," this "messenger of Satan" used, as he said, "to buffet me" (2 Corinthians 12:7).

Many people have attempted to determine what this "thorn" was, positing various ideas that seem plausible. I have my own suspicions regarding what it was, but, ultimately, they are all just guesses. We don't know because Paul didn't tell us. What we do know is that he struggled with it, whatever it was.

REMEMBER THE "PROMISE VS. PRINCIPLE" DISCUSSION?

So Paul prayed, possibly even begged, but what was God's answer?

Remember the "ask and ye shall receive" discussion in chapter 13? Paul's request came to God, God received it, weighed it against his perfect will for Paul's life, and determined that his answer would be quite different from what Paul had requested.

God often hears our prayers for what we desire, but in the end gives us what we need.

SOLOMON AND PAUL

Solomon was the recipient of some lavish gifts from God. Wisdom, of course, was the principal gift. It was the one that enabled him to be a good king.

Likewise, Paul was the recipient of some amazing gifts in terms of revelations and experiences from God, all of which equipped him to write the books of the Bible attributed to him, as well as to establish churches all over the then-known world.

How Did Solomon Handle It All?

As we have seen, Solomon was not a good steward of all that God gave him. He allowed the wonderful gifts he had received to have a negative, ultimately destructive effect on his life. He allowed the wisdom to become a burden to him. He became cynical and resentful of the weight of it all. He invested the riches in himself and his pleasure, none of which proved fulfilling to him. He allowed his worldwide fame and the adoration that most everyone had for him, including people in foreign lands, to cloud his judgment. This was due to the immense pride he developed in himself.

Women from all over the world and many other religions made themselves available to him. He took them as wives and concubines. Over time, these women persuaded him to honor their pagan gods with shrines, idols, and temples. Ultimately, these things combined to bring Solomon down. It was a sad ending to an amazingly blessed life.

Back to Paul

Paul's testimony as recorded in 2 Corinthians 12 is fascinating. I have referred to it over and over during the years of my ministry. In verses 1–10, Paul spoke of his inner conflict regarding this "thorn in the flesh." Though the temptation is great to delve into all ten verses, it would take longer than would be necessary for the purpose of this book.

Paul spoke of the amazing revelations and visions he received during the course of his Christian ministry. He even gave testimony, somewhat cryptically, of being caught up into a spiritual realm that no man had ever seen before. Although he spoke of this experience in the third person ("I knew a man in Christ . . . such an one caught up to the third heaven"—2 Corinthians 12:2), most everyone concurs he was speaking of himself. The New Living Translation says, "I was caught up to the third heaven." The point is that Paul had been given unspeakable revelations.

In verse 7, Paul seemed to say that he understood the purpose of this "thorn in the flesh." He realized the many revelations and lofty spiritual experiences afforded him could have caused him to be exalted in his own mind, so he wrote:

> *Lest I should be exalted above measure through the abundance of the revelations, there was given to me a thorn in the flesh, the messenger of Satan to buffet me, lest I should be exalted above measure.*
> 2 Corinthians 12:7

Although he seemed to recognize the reason for this "thorn," it remained difficult for him to endure, so he implored God to remove it from him.

Some may deem it cruel, but God had a specific purpose for this ongoing personal issue Paul had to deal with. God's answer to Paul's plea was that the thorn would be left in place. It was explained to Paul that it was a protection for him. By virtue of all that Paul had received and experienced in his outstanding ministry, the possibility that he would be exalted in his own mind was a dangerous reality. He could conclude that he was better, stronger, smarter, and more important than others. He could have had the same thing happen to him that happened to Solomon.

That pesky thorn was a continual reminder of his never-ending need for God and his grace. He had to remember that what he had was just given to him and that he needed God just like everyone else.

How Did God Answer Paul's Prayer?

> *And he said unto me, My grace is sufficient for thee: for my strength is made perfect in weakness.*
> 2 Corinthians 12:9

God assured Paul that his grace and favor would always be extended to him, bringing him strength and sustenance as well as the ability to cope with the struggle caused by this thorn. He further explained that Paul's weaknesses would be a greater source of glory to God than his strengths. Paul's intellect, his drive, and his commitment to the mission seemed to be a part of his make-up; thus, they were not the areas where he depended most upon God. It appeared he could always rely upon those personal traits as was demonstrated in his former life as a Pharisee.

God's grace and power are much more evident in the areas of our weaknesses. Areas where we struggle, where we are not so self-confident, where we do not shine so brightly on our own—they are the areas that are most glorifying to God when they are submitted to him.

His strength is made perfect and is most evident in *our weakness*.

Paul Understood

Fortunately, unlike Solomon, Paul did not become cynical. He did not develop a superior attitude because of his special revelations and experiences. Despite his intellect, his innate drive, and his extensive knowledge, he never forgot the main reason for whatever success he enjoyed.

> *But by the grace of God I am what I am: and his grace which was bestowed upon me was not in vain; but I laboured more abundantly than they all: yet not I, but the grace of God which was with me.*
>
> 1 Corinthians 15:10

As it was with the apostle Paul, so is it with us. Although *what* we know is important, it's *who* we know that makes the difference. Our hope is always in Jesus Christ and the grace he gives us every day. So the point of this chapter is to explain that although wisdom, understanding how things work, and knowledge of the word of God are all very important, they are not enough. We will always need a vital relationship with our gracious God. Regardless of how intelligent, wise, knowledgeable, and experienced we are, we never outgrow our need for him.

So let me repeat: Wisdom alone is not enough!

Please do not forget that.

~ Chapter 17 ~
THE BIG PICTURE

What is the difference between *micro* and *macro*? The term *micro* indicates scrutinizing something as if under a microscope, or as in the case of life, on a minute-by-minute basis. If a business owner or manager is known as a micromanager, it is because he or she wants to manage or dictate every little detail of the business. This may be possible and even necessary in a small business in which there are very few people who know enough about the business to make important decisions.

The term *macro* relates to what could be called *the big picture*. In understanding how things truly work, one must focus more on the big picture and less on a minute-by-minute or even day-by-day assessment. The larger the business, the less capable the upper-level manager would be to monitor every detail. In a large corporation the CEO (Chief Executive Officer) would need many managers under him/her who would be entrusted with running all the various departments in a way commensurate with the overall business model as adopted by the CEO and the board of directors.

In writing *That's Just the Way It Works*, the purpose is *not* to suggest that we all must live cookie-cutter lives doing everything alike. This is not some step-by-step instructional manual that tells us every move to make. We can live endless numbers of ways while remaining within the parameters of God's creational, natural laws. In other words, God allows us lots of latitude in how we live. In fact, he expects us to live life creatively, to use our amazing minds and imaginations to accomplish great things. It's just that when we incorporate the basic laws of God's natural creation, understanding what works and what does not, we create a flow of blessing that is very beneficial to us and those around us.

We all (and I do mean *all*) make mistakes. We all do things that end up backfiring on us. At times we do things unwittingly; at other times we do things even though we know better, hoping it will work out anyway. (You know the saying *You reap what you sow*? It is said that some young people go about sowing their wild oats while praying for crop failure.)

In reading this book, one could easily say, *Hey, I've done my best to live by God's principles, but I've had more than my fair share of trouble and heartache.* You may have done many things you thought were right only to be rewarded not with blessing, but with trouble, confusion, and disappointment.

The intention here is not to create the illusion that if one does all the right things nothing bad can ever happen. As I said, this is not a step-by-step manual or tutorial that will guarantee you the dream life. There are too many variables. Even if one person does all the right things (assuming that ever happens), not everyone else does. Thus, our lives are affected not only by what we do, but often by what others do also. This is the reason the big picture is so important.

People may attempt to create a flow of love, mercy, and forgiveness in their life only to find that others despise them and hold grudges against them. How's that for *give and it shall be given*? Of course, not everyone is loving, merciful, and forgiving, but over time the big picture ultimately will reveal that these traits truly do create a flow of these good things. A loving person will be loved. A merciful person will receive mercy. A forgiving person will be forgiven.

Looking at life minute by minute or day by day may not seem to show the truth of these principles, but eventually they always prove to be true. Why? Because that's just the way it works.

A Brief Pause for Further Explanation

I said earlier that God does not expect us to live cookie-cutter lives but to be creative.

This reminds me of a situation in Acts 15, which transpired during a time of critical disagreement among the leaders of the new church regarding the transition from Mosaic Law to the new dispensation of grace. A solution to the problem had to be determined and established. So they drafted a letter that would be circulated among leaders in outlying areas explaining their decision and stipulating that "it seemed good to the Holy Ghost, and to us" (Acts 15:28).

The church is, in a way, a joint venture between God and his people. Another indication of this is a verse which says,' and they went forth, and preached everywhere, the Lord working with them" (Mark 16:20). In still another place Paul referred to all of us as "workers together with him" (2 Corinthians 6:1), referring to God.

God has imparted his wisdom to us so we can know how to live our lives and conduct our affairs in a way that generates the flow of blessing through us. In the church as well as our individual lives we have lots of leeway in determining how to live in creative ways while maintaining the understanding of God's creation and how it works.

PUT AWAY THE MICROSCOPE

It can take a span of years to fully understand the benefits of living a life in accordance with Bible teaching. As I've said many times over the past few years, I can say certain things that no young person can say because I have the benefit of long years of experience by which to assess the results of a particular lifestyle. During any one short span of time, I may have concluded that the efforts I made to do what I thought was right didn't produce the positive results I expected. In fact, at times I've wondered if God knew where I was or even *who* I was. Nothing was going right. Everything seemed to be falling apart. It made no sense.

Job to the Forefront One More Time

Let's consider Job's situation one more time because his story and our story may have some striking, even instructive similarities.

Job was, according to God, perfect and upright. What happened? Everything bad that could happen did happen. (Remember Murphy's Law: "Anything that can go wrong, will go wrong"? Maybe that should have been called Job's Law.)

At one point, as Job was considering his pitiful circumstances, he declared, and I paraphrase, *I looked for God to my right, my left, in front of me, and behind me; I could not find Him anywhere* (See Job 23:8-9).

My interpretation of this scene is that Job could not see God in any of the horrible pain, loss, and grief he was suffering. How could this happen? God couldn't be in this!

Have you ever looked at your life and said the same thing: "God can't be in this!"

Yet amid this confusion Job found a glimmer of faith down deep in his soul—enough to declare, *I may not know where he is, but he knows where I am, and when I get through this, I'll be better than I was before,* (Job 23:10 Author's Paraphrase).

Then There Is David

> *I have been young, and now am old; yet have I not seen the righteous forsaken, nor his seed begging bread.*
> Psalm 37:25

David certainly had cause to wonder at times whether God was for him or against him. After all, it was nearly fifteen years from the time he was anointed to be the king of Israel before he actually ascended to the throne. During those years he spent most of his time fleeing for his life. It had to be confusing, frustrating, and challenging to his faith. He must have wondered if it was all a mistake. Did God truly intend for him to be the king? Was he, in fact, forsaken? Did the God he loved and worshiped care about him? I can't imagine David during all of the chaos saying, *Ah, I'm not worried. Everything will work out.* Take the time to go back and read about all that happened to him during those tumultuous years. It had to be overwhelming!

It would take years of life and times of reflection upon all that happened before David could realize that God was with him through it all. Even when it didn't seem so, God was there.

With all due respect to younger people (and I seriously mean that), the statement in the verse above, for the most part, can only be made by an older person with a broader perspective. An older person with lots of experience can view the bigger picture. Sometimes it just takes time for things to work out.

A minute-by-minute or day-by-day perspective could give us a very distorted picture of what God's grace looks like. Younger people have only a limited amount of time on this earth from which to draw conclusions regarding the workings of God in their lives, causing them to often think their efforts to do the right things do not produce good results.

This micro perspective not only affects younger people; it also can affect older people who can't see a bigger picture. Most of us are familiar with the mentality that says, *What have you done for me lately?* This can affect young and old alike. We all must remember God never promised that living for him would produce a life of constant bliss, wealth, and convenience. Living for God is still life, and life on this earth will always have its challenges. Don't ever forget that.

Another Brief Pause

Please understand that I really do love young people. So when I mention them and their inability to understand the long-term assessment of God's goodness in their life, it is not my intention to denigrate them in any way. Many young people are very thankful for God's grace even in trying situations. They need not necessarily wait for years to acknowledge that. It's just that a long-term view as experienced by older people gives us a greater range of life experiences by which to assess God's goodness in our lives.

I feel that I've always appreciated the goodness of God, but each passing year broadens my perspective regarding various twists and turns in my life, some of which were unforeseen and certainly unintended, and how they have fit into God's greater plan for me.

Many things happen in life that we find hard to interpret. Often, time is required for us to make sense of some of these things. "In your patience possess ye your souls." You know who said that, right? Of course, it was Jesus (Luke 21:19).

A CHAOTIC WORLD

Questions such as this are often asked, *If God is such a loving and good God, why is the world filled with disease, hunger, violence, hatred, crime, and such?* This question is often set forth as a repudiation of God rather than a desire for a plausible explanation. It is not unusual for people to ask questions like this rhetorically as if to say, *If I were God, things would be a lot different.* God addressed this issue with Job.

> *Wilt thou also disannul my judgment? Wilt thou condemn me, that thou mayest be righteous?*
> Job 40:8

The question put to Job is about people who criticize God regarding things like disease, hunger, natural catastrophes, and other unfortunate things that happen. It's as though, in their minds, a loving God would never allow those things to occur, and if it were up to them, they certainly would not. The question insinuates that their condemnation of God makes them more righteous than he is.

While all of us wish those bad things wouldn't happen, it is not about whether or not God is a good God. It is ultimately about a fallen world, which is what we are living in.

The questions are very simple, but the answers can be complicated. The simplest answer is that from the days of Adam and

Eve until now, humanity has largely ignored the wisdom of God in terms of the way creation works and instead favored its own ways. The consequences of that are and will always be chaos.

THE BIGGEST PART OF THE BIG PICTURE—ETERNITY

We said earlier that the natural creation is very similar to the spiritual world in the way it works. Many people make the mistake of thinking the spiritual world and natural world are vastly different and have little to do with each other. The assumption is that what one does in the natural world is completely separate from the spiritual world and therefore should be of no concern.

My view is that our natural lives in this world are simply lived in preparation for eternity. The wisdom God imparts and the understanding of how things work here are mainly for the purpose of getting us ready for the life to come.

When Jesus saved our souls, it was not just to give us wonderful, trouble-free, pleasurable, convenient lives here on earth. It was to prepare us for eternity where our rewards will be great. Not here.

Please don't think I'm saying we are to expect blessings to be given to us only in the afterlife while our lives on earth will be miserable. That's not the case! In the words of Jesus,

> *Verily I say unto you, There is no man that hath left house, or parents, or brethren, or wife, or children, for the kingdom of God's sake, Who shall not receive manifold more in this present time, and in the world to come life everlasting.*
>
> Luke 18:29–30

I know there is a lot to unpack in these verses, but the main thing I'd like you to notice is that decisions made in terms of following Jesus will result in blessing *in this present time,* **and** *in the world to come.*

This is part of what "The Big Picture" is about. It's not only about *time,* but also about *eternity.*

Understanding how things work is beneficial in generating a flow of blessing in our lives here on earth *as well as* in eternity, or, as Jesus said in the verse above, *in the world to come.*

IN CONCLUSION

God has given us ample opportunity to know how life works. The information is available through his word, but it also is available, to a certain extent, in the context of our lives.

The inhumanity of people to people is, sad to say, never ending. In families, businesses, schools, local governments, and even nations, efforts are made to control others, establish superiority, and to do so in any way possible. That is very sad.

On the other hand, God has given all of us the opportunity to know the benefits of living our lives in the wisdom of God. Realizing that life can take twists and turns we wouldn't expect, we also can know that rich rewards ultimately will accrue to those who follow his ways.

~ Chapter 18 ~
WISDOM FOR YOUR LIFE

This entire book is about biblical wisdom and its practical application in life. In the previous chapters we have looked at several areas of life that can be impacted by an understanding of how things tend to work in terms of God's creation. In this chapter I would like to be more specific. We will look at *your* life and how the wisdom we've been discussing can be applied to *you*. So the question here is, *How can an understanding of how life works be applied to your life individually?*

In studying human behavior, one inevitably encounters the phrase "nature versus nurture." The gist of this phrase is about what role nature plays in the development of an individual compared with the role of nurture. Nature refers mostly to genetic predisposition; that is, what a person does or becomes is due to natural, innate tendencies. Nurture is about what one does or becomes based upon environmental determinations.

NATURE

When God created the heaven and the earth, his wisdom provided a logical structure to it all. We call it nature. It is embedded in everything. Whether we are referring to the vast universe that stretches into infinity or the microscopic world of electrons, protons, and neutrons, the world—indeed the universe—works exactly the way

God intended. Human beings can observe it, study it, and theorize about its function, but they cannot change it.

Not to get too far beyond my limited expertise (which would be very easy to do), an observation of the animal kingdom reveals that nature is so embedded in the various species that each one behaves in certain, quite predictable ways.

One example comes to my mind that I have always found interesting. Have you ever considered all the various kinds of birds and the types of nests they build? A quick internet search will produce hundreds of pictures showing a vast variety of nests. They can be very small and simple or quite large and immensely complicated, depending upon what species of bird is building the nest. Go ahead, look it up. It's amazing. The point is, none of them took classes or attended seminars to learn how to build their particular type of nest; it was just in their nature.

Apparently, Solomon's observations were not only about human behavior, but they also included other areas of nature. In Proverbs 6:6–8, he admonished the "sluggard" to "go to the ant" and consider that despite "having no guide, overseer, or ruler," she displays an amazingly industrious approach to her existence. She instinctively stores up food in the summer for the long hard winter. She does this not because she was taught to do so, but because it is in her nature. The sluggard, or as he is referred to in various versions of scripture, *lazy fool, lazy bum, hater of work,* or *slothful one* to name a few, knows what he should do to make provision for himself, but he chooses not to do so. So even though we acknowledge human nature, we are not programmed to act in certain ways as animals, birds, and insects are.

NURTURE

My intention is not to enter into a lengthy discussion or debate with a psychologist about "nature versus nurture." My point is simple. The portion of God's creation that is unique—unlike any other—is humanity. Human beings are not "programmed" in the same way animals are. We all have a basic nature, but unlike animals, we have a wide, virtually unlimited range of possible ways to live and exist in this world.

We're talking about choice. Every human being is endowed with it. God did not create us to live like robots, programmed to function only in certain ways. He gave us minds, the ability to think for ourselves, imagination, and free will. We can think what we want, believe what we want, do what we want. If we choose to believe in God, we can. If we choose to deny his existence, we can do that too. Nature does not force us to do anything we don't want to do.

Nature does not predetermine what we do and how we do it, but our environment plays a major role in providing us with many choices. Our environment does not force us to do what we do or to think how we think; we always have a choice. At the same time, our environment, our culture, the way we were raised, what we were taught, and the examples that were lived out before us can all be powerful determinants involved in how we ultimately live.

HOW DOES THE NURTURE PART FIT IN WITH NATURE?

As we have said, there are right ways and wrong ways, good ways and bad ways to live. Some ways work well; others do not.

God gives us ample opportunity to know about his wisdom and how we can implement it to our advantage. Learning his ways and following in his paths tends to create blessing in our lives. Ignoring his ways and forging our own paths can lead us into a life of chaos, confusion, heartache, and pain.

When certain things about human nature are understood, they can be implemented in a very positive way. If, however, we allow the world's environment to nurture us in such a way as to steer us away from the wisdom of God, then we can find our lives tumbling into chaos.

THINK ABOUT THIS

Why is our world so filled with hate, anger, jealousy, depression, addiction, abuse, and killing? And that's just the short list.

Why are people so confused about who they are, what they are, whether there is any reason or purpose in life? Is our existence just a crazy quirk of fate? Are we, as humans, simply the result of some universal, unexplainable, cosmic accident?

Is there any reason at all to live our lives in "righteousness"? By the way, what is righteousness? Is it some random set of rules adopted by a bunch of powerful people to keep everyone in line and under their control?

What difference does it make what I do in this world? How I live my life? When I die, I'm just dead. That's it. Eventually all of us will be dead.

Whether it is a person who denies the existence of God altogether, or one who simply determines that God is some uninterested or uninvolved deity existing in some other realm, these questions are asked all the time.

WHAT AM I TRYING TO SAY HERE?

We have looked into several areas of life that we all experience, showing how we can live in positive, productive ways if we choose to live by the wisdom of God. Here are some of the subjects we've examined:

We looked at the wisdom of Solomon and how he acquired it.

We acknowledged that life is, or at least can be, hard, often involving difficult choices.

We examined the constant flow of everything in creation, showing how we can direct the flow of some positive things through our lives by what we do and how we treat others. Although none of this is discernable by physical calculations, it can be observed in the course of our lives.

We covered judgment and consequences.

We examined the make-up of a human being—spirit, soul, and body—even as it pertains to Jesus. In this discussion we attempted to explain the inner conflicts we all experience.

We asked ourselves several questions: How can a person overcome temptations and addictions? What is the difference between a promise and a principle? Is wisdom enough to enable living a successful life, or do we still require God's grace?

What about the big picture? Is everything so "cut and dried" and simple that it can be observed and understood on a day-by-day basis? No. Some of the ultimate blessings of a well-ordered life can take time, sometimes years, to fully realize.

THE MAIN POINT OF THIS CHAPTER

It has taken a while to get here, but this could be the most important chapter in the book. Of all of life's issues mentioned above (and we could have introduced many more), so much of the benefit of each one can depend on what this chapter is about—how we build our own personal lives.

THIS IS VITALLY IMPORTANT

> *The LORD by wisdom hath founded the earth; by understanding hath he established the heavens. By his knowledge the depths are broken up, and the clouds drop down the dew.*
> *Proverbs 3:19–20*

My reason for inserting these verses for the umpteenth time is so that you, the reader, can make an immediate comparison between it and the following passage.

> *Through wisdom is an house builded; and by understanding it is established: And by knowledge shall the chambers be filled with all precious and pleasant riches.*
> *Proverbs 24:3–4*

I trust you see the similarities. In the first example, we see the wisdom, understanding, and knowledge by which God created all things. In the second example, we see those same attributes applied to the building, establishing, and furnishing of our own house.

A Brief Pause for Explanation

Someone might say, *I thought the author said the Bible is not a book of one-liners, yet it seems he's placed undue emphasis on two verses: Proverbs 3:19–20.*

That's a valid point. The difference is that for my purposes these verses are just the starting point. They do not stand alone; they simply form the basis for my belief that the world created by God functions in the way he designed it to function. Whether or not the reader accepts my conclusions, for me these verses provide insight that causes many things to fall into place.

When I decided to undertake this project, my main purpose was to offer some simple yet plausible answers to some honest questions. Lots of people know what the Bible says—you know, the dos and don'ts—and out of a desire to be obedient, they attempt to follow the "rules." Unfortunately, many may not know why those things are important or even if they *are* important in and of themselves. My purpose is to show that God's instructions about life are not random or arbitrary. They are not given for the purpose of testing our willingness to subject ourselves to unexplainable laws and regulations simply to satisfy some obedience requirement. They have solid reasoning behind them. It is precisely that reasoning that I hope to have set forth.

WHAT IS A HOUSE? (Proverbs 24:3–4)

Good question. Is a house the physical domain in which we dwell? It could be, but that is not the primary application intended in these verses.

In the Bible, the word *house* often indicates a family; that is, fathers, mothers, children, grandchildren, great grandchildren, and on down the line. We find scriptural references to the house of Pharoah, the house of Levi, the house of Joseph, the house of David, and many more. None of these houses allude to a physical structure; they allude to a family.

Hence the instruction given regarding how we should build our families corresponds with the declaration regarding how God built the world in which we live.

Although we equate the house with a family, it must start with the individual. I cannot build my house, my family, on a firm foundation if I do not start with a firm foundation of my own. A well-grounded family starts with a well-grounded individual.

REMEMBER WHEN JESUS SAID THIS?

> *Therefore whosoever heareth these sayings of mine, and doeth them, I will liken him unto a wise man, which built his house upon a rock: And the rain descended, and the floods came, and the winds blew, and beat upon that house; and it fell not: for it was founded upon a rock. And every one that heareth these sayings of mine, and doeth them not, shall be likened unto a foolish man, which built his house upon the sand: And the rain descended, and the floods came, and the winds blew, and beat upon that house; and it fell: and great was the fall of it.*
>
> Matthew 7:24–27

Jesus was not giving a seminar on architecture; his instructions had to do with life. In these verses he speaks about the safety of a life and a family that are built on a firm foundation as opposed to ones built upon shifting sands. When the storms of life assail that house—that life, that family—the firm foundation provides strength and stability. Building on the principles of God's word provides continuity and permanence.

The wisdom of God has survived and will survive forever. It has been tried and proven for generations. Conversely, the wisdom of the world is unpredictable. It changes constantly.

As I write these words today, we are seeing a demonstration of this. Things that are considered natural, mainstream, unquestionably correct today are vastly different from the views and assumptions regarding many of those same issues just ten years ago. If you don't accept wholeheartedly what is being demanded today, you will be vilified, yet five years from now even that will have changed. That is the nature of the world's wisdom and philosophy.

How can you build a life on a foundation, a set of values you cannot count on for tomorrow? The answer is, oddly enough, you can, because you have the freedom to do so if you so choose. However, if you're looking through the same lens I am and seeing a society and a culture that is incredibly confused and disordered, you are not surprised. Neither am I.

BUILDING UPON A ROCK

As we have seen in Matthew 7, Jesus told us to build our house upon a rock and not upon the sand. He then informed us in Matthew 16 that he would build his church upon that same rock. Finally, Paul told us in 1 Corinthians 3 that his ministry was all about building on the foundation, which is Jesus Christ.

The rock spoken of in these references is "Jesus Christ [who is] the same yesterday, today, and forever" (Hebrews 13:8). The sand represents the shifting, ever-changing, completely unpredictable philosophies of the world.

Building on the firm foundation of the word of God means that you know what you believe and why you believe it. Your values, principles, and ideals are rooted, not only in the Bible, but in history. They have been tried and proven by many who have gone before you. They are reliable, predictable, and solid.

Building your life on the sand is like drifting aimlessly as a rudderless ship or floating as a feather on the wind. You cannot know where you will ultimately end up. You resign yourself to the whims of others, to the random thoughts and conclusions of people you don't even know and who don't know you. The questions you ask will be answered in concert with the philosophical music of the day. Ask the same questions tomorrow and, like people's favorite music choices, the answers will have changed drastically. You never know where you'll end up.

BUILDING ON A ROCK IS BUILDING ON THE TRUTH

Truth is not truth because I declare it. Truth stands completely alone, needing nothing or no one to prop it up.

Paul said in 2 Corinthians 13:8 that "we cannot do anything against the truth, only for it."

Meaning what? Meaning that the truth will stand regardless of whether we accept it, believe it, like it, declare it, doubt it, or whatever else we do regarding it. We can declare it, love it, live by it, and thereby provide a positive narrative regarding it, but even that will not change it. It cannot be enhanced, added to, detracted from, or altered in any way.

Some people refer to "my truth" as opposed to "your truth" as though we can have alternate truths. I can accept "my experience" versus "your experience," but neither my experience nor yours can in any way alter absolute truth. That is why we should seek to understand what truth is and to attempt to build our lives upon that truth.

A WONDERFUL CONTINUITY

I see in the two biblical selections above (Proverbs 3 and 24) a wonderful continuity regarding God's creation of the physical world and the instruction given regarding the building of our lives. When we observe the orderliness of the universe and the orderliness of nature, we can derive the understanding that if we attempt to abide by the same knowledge, understanding, and wisdom in ordering our lives, we can benefit greatly.

OKAY, SO WHAT IS TRUTH?

Remember when Jesus stood before Pilate, saying that he came into the world to bear witness to the truth, and that whoever is of the truth hears his voice? If so, you also will remember that Pilate's response to that was to ask the age-old question, "What is truth?" (See John 18:37-38)

Did you notice that Pilate didn't wait around for an answer? He asked the question and then walked away. Believe me, that happens a lot.

In another place, Thomas expressed a lack of understanding regarding Jesus' statements about believing in God, heaven, and his return to earth to take his people to be with him. Jesus continued, saying that where he was going, they knew, and the way, they knew. Thomas was confused; he didn't think that he knew the way, so he asked for clarification, Jesus said, "I am the way, the truth, and the life." (See John 14:4-6)

It is interesting to note that Thomas only asked about the way, but Jesus' answer was about the way, the truth, and the life. Notice that at the center of the way we all seek and the life we all desire to experience to the fullest, is the truth. I'm just saying . . .

I like that Thomas asked the question and, unlike Pilate, stayed to hear the answer. I wish many others would ask the same question today, not rhetorically but with a genuine interest in finding the answer.

CHOOSE YOU THIS DAY

I'll not tell the entire story; I'll just borrow a phrase from the book of Joshua. Joshua declared the direction that his family would go and implored the people of Israel to make their choice as well. His clarion call is immortal: *Choose you this day whom you will serve, the pagan gods of the world or the one true God* (Joshua 24:15 Author's Paraphrase).

There always is a choice. We can choose to believe or not believe, to serve or not serve. The foundation upon which we build is completely up to us.

My hope, my prayer, is that you will choose wisely to build upon the solid rock of the word of God, and that rock is Jesus Christ.

~ Chapter 19 ~

THE CONCLUSION OF THE WHOLE MATTER

Many phrases have been coined for the purpose of drawing a series of ideas, opinions, or thoughts to a conclusion. Here are a few:

> And the bottom line is . . .
> Just to wrap it up . . .
> And in conclusion . . .
> At the end of the day . . .

When attempting to explain what we think or believe, most of us will give several reasons for those beliefs and then attempt to consolidate all the reasons into a logical conclusion, sometimes using one of the above phrases.

SUMMARIZING SOLOMON'S STORY

Two Old Testament books are attributed mostly to Solomon—Proverbs and Ecclesiastes. In these two books Solomon's wisdom is on full display.

When Solomon became king, he asked God for wisdom that he might be a good leader of the people for whom he would be responsible. God granted him that request, but wisdom was not all he received. God also granted him the ability to become a very rich man.

As a result of his great riches, Solomon was uniquely capable of providing himself with virtually anything he desired. For the sake of brevity, I'll paraphrase how he described it.

> *I drank elegant wine. I performed great things: I built posh houses. I planted vineyards and elaborate gardens, and orchards with many varieties of trees. I even dug pools to irrigate the trees. I had more livestock than there had ever been in Jerusalem. And that's not all; I amassed silver and gold and a trove of interesting treasures.*
>
> *I had an abundance of servants, both men and women, who waited on me daily. Singers entertained me, both men and women. I called for every kind of musical instrument that struck my fancy. I availed myself of anything I wanted.*
>
> *As you might assume, I was great, the greatest that ever was. Surrounded by all of this, I was still able to maintain my wisdom. But when I surveyed all I had done, all I had amassed, the many people around me that catered to my every need and desire, I could only conclude that none of it mattered. All it amounted to was "vanity and vexation of spirit." There was no real value in any of it.*
> *– Author's paraphrase of Ecclesiastes 2:3–11*

Because Solomon had so much, he saw things that others would never see. One could say he saw things that he should not have seen, provided himself with things he should not have had, and experienced things he should not have experienced. He observed it all intensely and studied it closely. He determined cause and effect in terms of relationships and personal behavior based upon his vast experience. He was able to observe how life worked, the good and the bad. It all became the predominant subject of his writings.

The books of Proverbs and Ecclesiastes preserve the wisdom that Solomon accumulated over the course of his life, and especially during his time as king.

In the book of Ecclesiastes, one can deduce that Solomon, to some extent, became a bit pessimistic, even cynical. People who are very smart and highly educated sometimes may wish they did not know some of what they've learned along the way. It's as though all that knowledge can become too heavy a load. They can come to accept the phrase "ignorance is bliss" as true.

Maybe it is presumptuous of me to think that one can psychoanalyze Solomon simply by reading his writings. They certainly do give us insight into his thoughts about life, his attitudes, and the burdens he carried because of his gifts, but beyond that we cannot really know him. In our own experience, we can hear a lot about certain people—what they've accomplished, what leadership positions they've held, the writings they've published, or speeches they've given—only to find that when we actually meet them, they are quite different from what we had assumed. Such could be the case regarding Solomon.

Let me clarify that none of what I've said, either here or in previous chapters, is about judging Solomon. I'm not the judge; God is.

THE CONCLUSION OF THE WHOLE MATTER

We may all have opinions about some of the things Solomon did during his life and reign as king of Israel, but know this: it would be impossible to truly understand what it was like to be Solomon. How God regards the life and work of Solomon is solely his business. Solomon's life is an enigma, at least to me, but regardless of all his struggles he left us with an amazing understanding of life and how it tends to work.

If we read, study, and meditate upon the wisdom Solomon imparted in his writings and pray to God for guidance, we can order our lives in such a way as to avoid many of the pitfalls that a life lived foolishly can incur.

SOLOMON'S CONCLUSIONS

Solomon shared with the world many personal thoughts, ideas, revelations, interpretations, and even feelings in his writings. When it finally came time to "wrap it up" and state "the bottom line," here is what he wrote:

> *Let us hear the conclusion of the whole matter: fear God, and keep his commandments: for this is the whole duty of man.*
>
> *Ecclesiastes 12:13*

It's as though Solomon was saying, *I know this is a lot to process, but here's how I would sum it up. Everything I've said is important, but if you can just grasp this basic truth—fear God and keep his commandments—you've made a great start!*

Life will have its ups and downs. Not everything will work out as you thought it would or should. Even if you make all the best choices in life, you can't control everything. You do what you can and align yourself as closely to God's precepts as you know how, but you still must live with what others around you do. It's a complicated world; everyone knows that. Try as you may, you cannot understand everything.

What is important, though, is that you put your faith and trust in the one who ultimately will step in and take control, the one who in the end will make everything right. That, of course, is God.

In the meantime, heed Solomon's final word in the book of Ecclesiastes as he sets forth the admonition regarding the most important aspect of your life on this earth. *Fear God, and keep his commandments.* That is what it's all about.

~ Chapter 20 ~
AND FINALLY...

I have never written a book; that is, until now. I confess it is much more difficult than I thought it would be. And in my case, it's taking way more time than I expected.

Some say that authors should just write their book and publish it, that they shouldn't go back over it time and time again because they will just keep finding ways to change it. Others say that rewriting is the key to good writing. I don't know.

What about all the rules of punctuation, the use of italics, quotation marks, commas, semi-colons? Did I get them all right? No. I tried, but I'm sure that it's not to the liking of real editors. (I just think that in some cases, I know better. Just kidding!) I do hope that readers will overlook the errors.

Then there is the element of content. What should be included? What should be left out? Is the text too wordy? Does it ramble? Is it too complicated? Too simplistic? What about too much repetition? Are too many things said too many times? Does the author stay on point?

At what point does an author feel he has made his point? Do I keep writing because I feel the book is too short? Or maybe it's too long. I don't know.

All these questions and many more flood my mind. Too many of them still remain unanswered.

Too much information? Probably. Sorry—I'm bad about that.

SUCH A DILEMMA

Regarding speaking, not writing, someone once said, *If in thirty minutes you don't strike oil, stop boring.*

Whoa! That's harsh. I think I prefer a different analogy. A good friend of mine, an elder, once gave me some good advice regarding how long to stay and when to go. He said,

> *Always leave with them wanting you to stay; never stay with them wanting you to leave.*

Fully realizing that such advice has nothing to do with writing a book, I felt that with some creative manipulation I could make the phrase work for my purposes here. Here is the result of my edit.

> *Always stop with them wanting you to continue; never continue when they've had enough.*

A bit awkward? Maybe, but it has enabled me to conclude that I've arrived at that point. A lot more could be said, but I feel I've said enough.

IN CLOSING

May the God of heaven and earth, Jesus Christ, the creator of all that exists, bless all who read these words. May they expand your understanding and thereby bring encouragement to you as you navigate through this world on your way to eternity. And may that eternity be spent with our Lord Jesus Christ.

Thank you for reading, and God bless.

Printed in the USA
CPSIA information can be obtained
at www.ICGtesting.com
JSHW022245160823
46690JS00001B/4